To Cisco —

FACE TO FACE
with sports legends

JOE CULLINANE

Hope you all enjoy these nostalgic journeys.

Best wishes,
Joe Cullinane

Denver, Colorado

JaDan Publishing
PO Box 22198
Denver, CO 80222

Copyright © 2002 by Joe Cullinane
All rights reserved, including the right to
reproduce this book or portions thereof in
any form.

ISBN 0-9703197-1-1

Book design by Donna Murphy
Cover photo by Grant Leighton

Printed in the United States of America

TESTIMONIALS

"Joe Cullinane has interviewed them all; good guys, bad guys, role models, heroes and jerks. Now he brings them to life in this funny, no-holds-barred look at the people who make the games go. If you want to find out what being a sportscaster is all about and what makes sports stars tick, this book is for you."
~ *Jeff Kingery, Colorado Rockies broadcaster and former Denver Nuggets voice*

From the tip of the Rockies to the tropics of Florida, Joe Cullinane takes you on a kaleidoscopic journey through the eyes of a sports broadcast journalist. Joe D., The Mick, Reggie, The Earl of Baltimore, Dempsey, Marciano, Magic Johnson, Gretzky, Montana, Jackie Robinson and Red Barber are just a few of the passing parade Joe has interviewed. Cullinane has survived knockdowns to give you a bird's-eye view. His book possesses the sweet allure of nostalgia. But most of all, it's very very funny.
~ *Larry Dierker, former Houston Astros' manager, former broadcaster and former major league pitcher*

"If life experiences were the measure of a man's wealth, then longtime sports broadcaster, Joe Cullinane, would be listed in the Forbes 400. For every Bob Costas, Al Michaels or Dick Enberg, Joe represents the thousands who have dreamed, but never got the big break. But instead of any bitterness, he has taken nearly 50 years of memories and shared it with the reader. His list of interviewees reads like a

book of *Who's Who In Sports*. If you love sports, you'll love this book. It should be required reading at every Sportscasters Camp in America."
> ~ Dave Campbell, ESPN baseball analyst, former Colorado Rockies telecaster and former major league infielder

"Joe Cullinane weaves a fascinating story covering games on diamonds and fields on the high school, college and professional levels. His incredible recollection of Hall of Famers, zany characters, those who didn't make it, and those whose names will live in sports history forever, brings them all to life. In this wonderful business of sportscasting, Joe's career reflects the peaks and valleys all of us have experienced. It's a wonderful read!"
> ~ Harry Kalas, Philadelphia Phillies announcer—30 years, Houston Astros' announcer—6 years, NFL Films—20 years and Notre Dame Football television announcer—6 years. Also inducted into the Baseball Hall of Fame, 2002

"A person would be hard pressed to find a more knowledgeable broadcaster in the game of baseball than Joe Cullinane. He has been in the inner circle of America's pastime for more than four decades and shares experiences from some of the greatest events in the game. Joe has interviewed many of today's brightest stars."
> ~ Bob Gebhard, former Senior Vice President/General Manager, Colorado Rockies

"Joe Cullinane is a treasure. In over 40 years as a grass roots sportscaster, Joe has demonstrated a passion for his profession that is rare. His love of sports is evident as he takes you to a variety of venues where he worked. You'll meet Earl Weaver, Cal Ripken Jr., and many others. In this era, when agents, contracts and labor disputes have such a prominent role in sports, it is refreshing to hear a voice like Joe's. He loves what he does and that passion for his profession is evident in this entertaining book."

~ *Pete Van Wieren, Atlanta Braces broadcaster*

"The excerpts I've read from *Face to Face with Sports Legends* reflect Joe's keen understanding of how players view the game. His tales of their joys, heartbreaks and insecurities will enlighten fans everywhere."

~ *Al Hrabosky, the "Mad Hungarian," former major league pitcher and now St. Louis Cardinals' broadcaster*

"Baseball has been, without question, the most written about sport of all time. Now comes a book about baseball that is unique. Joe has put on paper his stories and anecdotes of players, teams, and personalities of the game based on his career as a broadcaster. It is a veritable travelogue of Joe's stops along the baseball trail. Mixed in is good advice for young sportscasters from the best of them. I've known Joe for 31 years, and believe me, no one could write a more interesting book."

~ *Marty Brennamann, Cincinnati Reds broadcaster—29 years, World Series broadcasters, 1975, 1976 & 1990. Baseball Hall of Fame inductee, 2000*

"One of the things I look forward to each time I come to Denver, is what I know will be an informative and enthusiastic interview with my friend, Joe Cullinane. Few people bring the love and excitement to an interview like Joe. I always look forward to an insightful exchange with Joe."

~ *Tom Glavine, Atlanta Braves pitcher, winner of two Cy Young Awards and MVP of the 1995 World Series*

"Joe Cullinane is to play-by-play sports broadcasting, what Otis is to elevators."

~ *Rick Reilly, Senior Writer, Sports Illustrated and winner of National Sports Writer-of-the-Year Award*

DEDICATION

My story and this book are dedicated to my beloved wife, Ottie. With unwavering willingness through both joyous and harsh times, she has endured with the relentless insecurities of the play-by-play announcing world as I have experienced it. With unshakable loyalty, she has steadfastly joined me on my roller coaster ride, always encouraging me to pursue my dreams.

Our sons Pat and Mike and daughter Susie have shared in the good times, but equally important, they, like Ottie, have been with me through the difficult days when one of the biggest challenges was to fight off discouragement. They are an exceptionally significant part of this book.

ACKNOWLEDGEMENTS

I thank Jan Sumner and Jeff & Meryl Kingery for painstakingly critiquing my work and for their steadfast belief in my story.

To Lyn Wazny, a treasured friend, for her cheerful contribution of countless hours and concentrated effort in computerizing the entire manuscript.

Many thanks to Gerry Mellman, a dedicated and talented sports photographer, who voluntarily and enthusiastically took many of the pictures that appear in this book.

For Tom Gleason, a wonderful gentleman, who first suggested I write this book.

Mark Rucker, who also insisted and contributed to the writing of this book.

Thanks to Vic Boccard, who constantly lent encouragement with his time and creative ideas.

Last and certainly not least, to all the wonderful, interesting, eccentric, and amusing athletes, both past and present, that made this book possible.

CONTENTS

Foreword

1. The Journey Begins 1
2. My Career Takes Off 11
3. The Roundball Marathon 19
4. Keep Those Bags Packed 25
5. Show Me The Money? 35
6. Another Move—Same Old Challenge 45
7. The Roller Coaster—Plunges Downward 51
8. From Billy Martin To Ted Williams 65
9. A Sad Time In The Life Of A Great Coach 77
10. Fond Memories Of Harry, Red, Mel & Hornsby 87
11. At Long Last, A Chance To Advance 99
12. Characters Of The Games 111
13. Battling For My Job 121
14. Pinch-hitting For Hank Aaron 131
15. My Big Chance 137

CONTENTS (Cont'd)

16. Picking Up The Pieces 149
17. Sojourn In The Sun 159
18. Charlie O. 169
19. Please Pass The Cough Syrup 177
20. Manager Merry-Go-Round And A Big Move 187
21. From "The Bullies" To "The Doctor" 197
22. DiMaggio, Mantle And The Shot 207
23. Montana, Reeves, Madden And A Few Other Football Notables 219
24. Stay Alert And Be Ready To Duck 227
25. Renewing An Acquaintance With Don Baylor 233
26. Knucklers And Knuckleheads 243
27. Mr. Nobody And Mr. October 249
28. The Business Of Broadcasting 255
Epilogue 263

FOREWORD

"Tell me another."

That's what I feel like saying whenever I have the good fortune of spending time with Joe, whether personal or professional.

He's one of the great storytellers I have ever been around, and that's how his book reads. *Face to Face With Sports Legends* is largely anecdotal in nature, and saying that Joe knows a lot of stories is a little like saying there's a lot of coffee in Brazil.

The stories never stop; stories that span years, personalities, and the games themselves. Joe has done play-by-play in five sports at all levels and his keen memory and insight make for wonderful reading.

When I read the manuscript, two things jumped out at me. First, the stories, so many of which were amusing and told in a way that reminded me of sitting around a fire listening to a favorite friend regale us with tales of where he'd been and what he'd seen. Second, his book is a microcosm of life. Good times, bad times, but always the richness of the journey.

Joe's own career provides the tapestry into which these stories are woven, complete with all the ups and downs that fifty-plus years as a broadcaster can provide.

To his credit, Joe never dwells on the dark side of sports or broadcasting, he has too much integrity for that, and believes the game's the thing; playing it, watching it and describing it.

There are a lot of books written by and about famous people. Sometimes their themes revolve around the authors of the celebrity. We have here, however, a guide whose legend lies in his ability to observe, record and pass along the stories that make a career, a career in which the writer answered the bell every day for 50 years. We are the richer for it.

Whether you're an avid fan, aspiring sportscaster, or just a casual observer of life, this is an entertaining and nostalgic read. With this sage veteran as your tour guide, you'll never be bored, and you too might find yourself asking, "Joe, tell me another."

Jim Saccomano
Director of Media Relations
Denver Broncos

1 THE JOURNEY BEGINS

Like countless other kids during the depression years, I didn't have the financial wherewithal to purchase entry into the hallowed grounds of Wrigley Field and Comiskey Park. That, however, was hardly an insurmountable obstacle. Blue Valley Dairy products frequently sponsored youth groups who would be allowed to sit in the lower left field stands at Comiskey Park. Sometimes I could unobtrusively slip into one of the lines as they entered the ballpark.

One warm summer day, when the White Sox hosted the World Champion Yankees, I couldn't refrain from testing my luck. Just as I was about to enter the park, a supervisor hollered, "He can't go in! He's not with our group!"

An over vigilant policeman drew back his nightstick and pummeled me black and blue. I remember shedding a few tears, not because of the beating, but because I was so close to seeing the Sox against the Yankees. Despite this experience the first seeds of desire were planted in me to become part of the wonderfully captivating game of baseball.

My entrée was the Junior Sportswriters' Contest of 1937, open to all boys ages 14-16. I became aware of the contest when I delivered newspapers for the Chicago Times. The format was simple. Each contestant had to submit an essay of approximately 250 words describing, "The greatest baseball play I ever saw." The Times was one of five daily newspapers in the Windy City.

I focused on a triple play I'd seen in a major league game. As I reconstructed the play in my Chicago Times story, I can't recall any difficulty in meeting the 250 words required as part of the contest's ground rules.

Each day the paper selected six contestants. Those six were either sent to Wrigley Field or Comiskey Park, to cover that day's game, depending on whether the Cubs or the White Sox were playing at home. The aspiring young writers would pose as a group for a Times photographer. Each day, a winner was selected from the group of six and that boy's story, along with his picture, ran in the next day's Times sports section. I was overwhelmed with joy when I saw my story and picture as that day's winner.

My group of six covered a game pitting the White Sox against the mighty New York Yankees with Joe DiMaggio, Lou Gehrig, Lefty Gomez, Bill Dickey, Tony Lazzeri and George Selkirk, who only two years earlier had succeeded Babe Ruth as the Yankees right fielder. Red Ruffing, who had toes missing on one foot as the result of an accident, was the Yankees' starting pitcher. The White Sox forged a ninth inning rally to overtake New York, 9-8. Tony Piet's single brought in future Hall of Famer Luke Appling with the winning run. I don't remember the Yankees being too upset. They were a runaway pennant winner en route to four straight world championships under stern taskmaster, Joe McCarthy.

CHAPTER 1: THE JOURNEY BEGINS

As the Times contest developed, each day's winner competing with all the others, the newspaper announced that the winner at season's end would cover the World Series. In 1937, that meant a trip to New York to cover the "Subway Series" between the Yankees and Giants. You can imagine the excitement I felt as the days dwindled down to the end of September. As with most 14-year-olds, my hopes ran extremely high.

At long last the announcement came. The winner was…Harry Butchin? His story, written months previously, was reprinted in the Times. It centered around an outstanding game pitched by the White Sox' Vernon Kennedy. Kennedy had chalked up 20 victories the previous year, but slumped badly in 1937. Young Butchin's imaginative lead read: "A ghost - the ghost of Vernon Kennedy of 1936, returned to Comiskey Park yesterday afternoon and…." I can still see the Times headline etched in my mind forever: (Butchin Winner, Covers Big Series.)

I was heartsick that I hadn't won, but just a day later I was surprised to read the Times would select two additional participants to cover the Chicago City Series, which took place annually between the Cubs and White Sox, in a best of seven showdown, same format as the World Series. I was one of the two chosen. My parents, who had baseball backgrounds, were extremely proud of me.

My mother grew up in a Libertyville, Illinois orphanage and on weekends she would often be permitted to go to Chicago and work as a vendor, hawking her wares through the stands at Comiskey Park. She met White Sox players and one, pitcher Joe Benz, invited her to be a flower girl at his wedding. My mother delighted in the atmosphere of a ballpark, but was not the slightest bit interested in the game itself.

Once, when they were attending a game together, my dad observed that the White Sox bullpen was getting busy, my mother questioned, "Why are they warming up a pitcher? Isn't it hot enough out there?"

My dad was a catcher on the St. Louis sandlots, as his gnarled fingers attested to. For the princely sum of 15 cents, he would sit in the Sportsman's Park grandstand to watch the Cardinals and Browns. He told me about seeing so many of baseball's early legends, Ty Cobb, Walter Johnson, Eddie Collins, Tris Speaker, and Honus Wagner.

He was so distraught at watching his beloved Cardinals get steamrolled by the Yankees in the 1928 World Series, a New York sweep, that he couldn't bear to watch when Babe Ruth and Lou Gehrig went on a home run binge that buried the Redbirds. Departing prematurely, my dad missed the chance to be an eyewitness at one of the more famous World Series games. As he had done in another game, the "Bambino" belted three homeruns that day. The only other player to blast three round trippers in a World Series game was Reggie Jackson, New York's "Mister October."

The Times had a clever approach to City Series coverage by its youthful scribes. By design, I would pitch my story to White Sox fans and my compatriot, Bernard Teitel, would slant his stories in favor of the Cubs. All objectivity was put aside. I became "Scuttlecubs" Cullinane, opposing "Throttlesox" Teitel. We waged fierce daily literary warfare. Before the series, sports editor Marvin McCarthy had us pose for a picture in which I was about to throw a punch while Bernard countered by hammering me with his typewriter.

Those were exciting days. I remember stepping onto the hallowed grass of Comiskey Park and Wrigley Field, venturing into dugout and clubhouse areas, hanging around batting cages, and getting acquainted with players. The first White Sox player I saw was third base coach Billy Webb. He promptly inquired, "Aren't you the kid whose picture I saw in today's Times?"

After my quick comeback of "Uh huh," Webb turned to pitcher "Sugar" Cain and said, "I told you I was a good detective." Webb then suggested I head for the clubhouse and introduce myself to manager Jimmy Dykes, who immediately made me feel at home.

I visited with future Hall of Famers Luke Appling and Ted Lyons and other famous stars including Luke Sewell, Zeke Bonura, Monty Stratton, Jackie Hayes and Dixie Walker, who would one day become the "People's Cherce" in Brooklyn. Years later, after blindness overtook Hayes, Walker informed me that Jackie was so despondent over the loss of his sight, that he unsuccessfully attempted to commit suicide - three times. Imagine, the feeling of an athlete with eyesight so incredibly keen, only to have a world of darkness close in. Sadly, two others, outfielder "Moose" Solters and pitcher Howie Judson would also lose their sight. A hunting accident ended Monte Stratton's career, which was later made into a movie starring Jimmy Stewart as Monte Stratton.

I met only one White Sox player toward whom I formed an immediate dislike, pitcher Johnny Rigney, who voiced sarcastic, negative comments about my writing. If I'd been quicker on the draw, I'd have snapped back that my writing was far better than his pitching. But what 14-year-old would react that way to the verbal abuse from a big leaguer? Rigney later became a White Sox front office executive as a result of marrying Dorothy Comiskey, granddaughter of the team's founder, Charles Comiskey.

Comiskey was such a tightwad, that eight of his players betrayed him and loyal Sox fans by selling out to gamblers and throwing the 1919 World Series. They would live in infamy as the "Black Sox," banned from organized baseball forever.

The 1937 Cubs were led by Hall of Famers Gabby Hartnett and Billy Herman, along with Stan Hack, Frank Demaree, Augie Galan and pitching ace, Bill Lee. It was sheer heaven, meeting the players, covering the game, then going back to the Times office each day to compose the game story. I honestly felt a letdown when the series, stretched to its seventh game, came to an end with "my team" victorious.

I rode streetcars either from home or school to the ballpark. One day, my railway companion was the aforementioned pitching standout, Vernon Kennedy. The fare was seven cents. It struck me years later, what a far cry from modern day millionaire ball players, driving their expensive vehicles to the ballpark.

When the City Series ended, Marvin McCarthy promised both Bernard Teitel and me that someday when we "came of age" he would bring us back as Times copy boys. For me, that meant becoming a part of the newspaper business would be at least four years away. I still had most of high school

CHAPTER 1: THE JOURNEY BEGINS

ahead of me. Once I graduated and entered Woodrow Wilson Junior College, I wrote sports for the school paper, and eventually became Sports Editor.

I remember one funny incident involving one of the first football games I covered there. Wilson was prepared to do battle with arch – rival, Orville Wright Junior College. Players were keyed up as they took the field for the showdown battle on a gray, gloomy Windy City November day. There was a biting chill in the air with snowflakes flying.

One player, Hubert Hood, who later became a Golden Gloves heavyweight boxing champ, turned pro and even fought an exhibition match with Joe Louis, decided to indulge himself with a bit of extracurricular fun and provide the fans with some pre-game entertainment.

He was almost fully attired in standard gridiron gear, including shoulder pads and kneepads, except for one conspicuous difference. In that bleak, wintry setting, Hood substituted a summer straw hat for his customary helmet. Fans howled as he trotted around the field with the brim bouncing. It must have had a positive affect on the team…they won.

A fellow junior college sports writer, Jay Wigoda, was obsessed by "Whirlaway", the top thoroughbred racehorse of 1942. Jay once disdainfully told his current lady friend, "I'd rather look into Whirlaway's eyes than yours," thereby killing a budding romance.

More than four years after Marvin McCarthy's promise following the 1937 City Series, I was hired by the Times as a copy boy while attending junior college at age 18. Many fledgling newspaper people took that very same route before becoming fulltime writers.

I was only a copy boy, but right from the beginning Sports Editor, Gene Kessler and assistant, Irv Kupcinet assigned me to write minor sports stories and to rewrite material mailed to the newspaper.

One day a week I would pinch-hit for handicapper, Ann Joy (wife of Marvin McCarthy, who had been elevated to Managing Editor). I worked under the pseudonym of Ann Joy and learned to handicap horse races for the Times turf section.

One day, on a trip to the nearby "Racing Form", I visited with Clem McCarthy. That famous gravelly voice was exciting even in conversation. McCarthy's specialties were boxing and horse racing. He announced many of Joe Louis' championship bouts and could make your spine tingle with his exciting Kentucky Derby descriptions.

My stint with the Times lasted less than a year because I was inducted into the army in January 1943. During World War II, I was assigned to an anti-aircraft battalion.

My successor at the Times was Jerome Holtzman, who eventually became an outstanding big league baseball writer, then a columnist. He authored (No Cheering in the Press Box) and first conceived the idea of "saves" for pitchers.

Following my discharge from the army, I attempted to enroll at Northwestern University, then Marquette, hoping to pursue a degree in journalism. It didn't work out, so I used the GI bill and enrolled at Columbia College and took a nine-month course in radio.

CHAPTER 1: THE JOURNEY BEGINS

Early in 1947, after completing the course, I set about searching for a job. I sent many letters to Midwest stations and connected with WSOY in Decatur, Illinois. My audition was a baseball re-creation simulated from the studio.

When I was breaking into radio, minor league announcers rarely traveled with their teams. A re-created game involved taking a pitch-by-pitch report supplied by Western Union. Then the announcer in the studio would expand on the report to make the game come alive. The broadcast would be further enhanced with sound effects including crowd noise, the crack of the bat and even the sound of vendors hawking their wares.

Never having attempted such an assignment previously, I felt extremely nervous and very much alone, but nevertheless talked for perhaps a full hour as the station recorded my re-creation.

Fortunately, I had listened to many of these re-creations. At one time in the late thirties, five Chicago stations would cover the same game, whether it be Cubs or White Sox contests. I could change the dial and get an interesting variety of different broadcasters. Because each station typically had two broadcasters, in a single afternoon I could conceivably listen to ten different announcers.

Following my Decatur audition, a decidedly unfriendly program director, Bernie Johnson, bluntly informed me, "You don't have good microphone technique." I didn't bother to ask him what he was talking about. I had never heard that expression before.

Two days later I received a telegram from station owner-general manager, Merrill Lindsay, informing me that he wished to hire me. In a matter of weeks my life in radio broadcasting was under way. First, however, I had to complete another assignment.

While I was attending radio school, I worked part time for the Chicago American Gears of the National Basketball League, a forerunner of the NBA. I would do stories for various press services and also phone in game stories and box scores to out-of-town newspapers. One of Chicago's players was the towering George Mikan, who recently had been voted the top pro basketball player of the first half-century.

I recall making an automobile trip to Indianapolis for a game, accompanied by two team officials. After the game, our driver became intoxicated, so I refused to make the return trip back to Chicago with him. I was sitting in the lobby of the Hotel Claypool. One of the players, Dick Triptow, asked me why I hadn't gone back to Chicago. When I explained the situation, he said, "Room with me. The other bed is too small for George," referring to the 6'11" Mikan. I gladly accepted his offer.

Our sleep, however, was interrupted at least three times during the wee hours, because George, would solicitously come into the room, turn on the lights and ask how we were sleeping. Triptow was furious but I didn't particularly mind. Mikan's bed was far more comfortable than the lobby chair I would otherwise have occupied.

The station didn't pay me enough to afford my own room.

2 MY CAREER TAKES OFF

I moved from Chicago to Decatur, about two weeks before the start of the 1947 Three I League (Illinois, Indiana, Iowa) season. It was one of the oldest leagues in professional baseball. A station announcer told me Harry Caray was once a broadcast applicant at WSOY, but flunked the audition because the station manager didn't feel his gravelly voice was suitable... and where's that guy today?

How does recreating a baseball game work? Well, here's an example of what might come over the wire:

First inning, Colorado up -

Young: Strike one, swinging. Ball one, low. Out, grounded to short.
Kingery: Ball one, high.- Strike one, swinging - Hit, line drive single to right.
Bichette: Foul back, strike one - Ball one, inside- Double to right, Kingery scores. Runner beat second baseman's relay throw on close play at plate.

> Galarraga: Strike one, called. Ball low, catcher makes diving stop in dirt to hold Bichette at second. All out, Galarraga lined to short and Bichette was doubled up attempting to get back to second.

One run, two hits, no errors, none left.

It's easy to see why a broadcaster's imagination must be given full play while doing a re-creation. For every minute of information sent, the play-by-play man must stretch his description many times over.

What about the sounds of the game? When I re-created games from the Rochester, New York studios, we would use a long crowd noise reel of tape. It was recorded before a game at Yankee Stadium. When it was time to up the crowd noise level, I would cue my engineer using hand signals to indicate how high the noise level should be. The engineer needed to pay close attention to my instructions. Obviously the crowd response would be vastly different when calling an RBI single, than a three-run homer.

After extensive experimentation, we hit upon just the right combination of tools to simulate the sound of a bat hitting a ball. I would whack a ruler against a hockey puck to produce the desired effect. Hey, whatever works!

There is a certain rhythm a broadcaster must maintain for an effective re-creation. It's vital not to talk too fast or too often. We let the crowd noise take over so we didn't overwhelm our listeners. And we made sure not to invent excite-

CHAPTER 2: MY CAREER TAKES OFF

ment when it wasn't there. The key was, I had to imagine I was actually there.

How difficult was it to do an effective re-creation? Let's just say it's much tougher than a live broadcast. Before long your mind wanders. Having to concentrate on giving a realistic, detailed account of a contest you're not even watching is challenging, to say the least.

I remember one stretch in Rochester when I re-created eight games in four nights! There were four straight International League double headers that were played in Jacksonville, Florida. Three of the eight games went into extra innings. I sat in a studio, working alone one night talking for six and one half hours straight; frequently doing live commercials between innings.

The best tribute a listener can pay the re-creating announcer is to tell him, "I could have sworn you were at the game."

1947 was a memorable summer. I broke into radio and broadcast my first season of baseball. The Decatur Commodores, a St. Louis Cardinals' affiliate, who were incredibly inept, finished 17 games out of seventh place in an eight-team league. They won 28 of 126 games! They were embarrassingly creative in inventing new and unique ways to lose. I did see many opposing players who would eventually distinguish themselves in the major leagues. Carl Erskine, Decatur's pitching opponent in the season opener, would one day become a Brooklyn Dodgers' World Series hero, once striking out 14 New York Yankees.

I described the play of Johnny Logan, who became the Milwaukee Braves' shortstop on their 1957-58 World Series teams. Logan's manager at Evansville in 1947 was Bob Coleman. Coleman previously managed the Boston Braves, but he preferred working with eager minor league hopefuls who welcomed his teaching expertise.

The old adage, "You can't tell the players without a scorecard," certainly held true for that 1947 Decatur team. Sixty players passed through the team's constantly revolving door.

Waterloo, Iowa produced six players who eventually became major leaguers with the White Sox. They switched managers despite having a solid playoff-bound ball club. Such a change was most unusual in the lower minors. The new skipper, Jack Onslow, didn't want the assignment. He grumbled to me about "Always having to keep your bags packed in this ridiculous game." Ironically, two years later he was elevated to the Chicago White Sox managing post. I wondered later if he still felt the same way.

Decatur had one outfield prospect in 1947 who earlier achieved fame on the basketball court. He was Andy Phillip, who captained the legendary "Whiz Kids" at Illinois University. Phillip later became a player and head coach in the NBA. Another Decatur player also had a strong basketball background. He was first baseman Ed Mickelson, who played for coaching immortal Hank Iba at Oklahoma A & M, as it was then known. Mickelson did reach baseball's big leagues for a short time, playing for both the Cardinals and Browns.

Davenport, Iowa's manager was Dickie Kerr. A familiar name, he won two games for the infamous "Black Sox" in the fixed World Series of 1919. In the late thirties, in Daytona Beach, Florida, Kerr managed a hard-throwing, wild, teen-

CHAPTER 2: MY CAREER TAKES OFF

age pitcher. The youngster hurt his arm diving for a sinking line drive, and was then pressed into service as an outfielder. Kerr liked the way the lad swung the bat and coaxed him into becoming an everyday player, sore arm and all. The player was Stan Musial. Musial's regard for Kerr was so great that he named his first son Dickie.

My booth in Decatur wasn't separated from the press box. That presented no problem unless a mean-spirited, cantankerous sports columnist named Howard Millard happened to be in a particularly venomous mood. If that were the case, listeners would be apt to hear a bellowing voice exclaiming, "What are you talking for? No one's listening, anyway." What a wonderful and clever guy!

While the Decatur ball club plunged ever deeper into the Three I League cellar, crowds predictably dwindled until we couldn't tell the vendors from the fans. One night, after recapping the game and concluding my broadcast, I sauntered toward the "Fans' Field" exit gate. Had I been aware of what awaited me when I attempted to leave, I would have quickened my post-game routine. There wasn't a fan, vendor, player or security guard in sight. The place was as dark as the inside of an underground mineshaft. I had gotten locked in!

It would be far into the wee hours of the following morning before a security guard finally appeared, to free me from my imprisonment in that mausoleum.

Another night, sitting alongside a Western Union Morse code operator in the studio while re-creating a road game, I was startled by an unannounced, but welcome visitor, Sally Rand.

Sally gained no small measure of fame when she performed as a fan dancer at the Century of Progress World's Fair in Chicago in 1933. Sally had the well-deserved reputation of developing fan dancing into a fine art. The fans covered her entire anatomy, so she couldn't be accused of indecent exposure while whirling gracefully around the dance floor. I can't recall how Sally was attired the night she visited me, but I do know the famous fans weren't part of her getup. She had performed her act earlier in the evening at a carnival near the ballpark, and decided to stop by, appropriately enough, "Fan's Field."

Another experience really jolted me and caused considerable consternation. It happened on a warm, humid midsummer night. I was re-creating the pitch-by-pitch story of a Decatur road game in the studio. Station policy prohibited use of a fan and, of course, it was long before air conditioning. The air was miserably heavy. The Western Union operator left the studio temporarily, leaving me all alone. No problem, I normally worked about half an inning behind the Western Union report anyway.

With Decatur absorbing another drubbing I began to relax and before I knew what happened my eyelids closed.

Suddenly I heard a voice whispering in my ear, away from the microphone, "Joe. Joe! Come on Joe! Wake up!"

Quickly, horrifyingly, it dawned on me. I had dozed off during my own broadcast! All the listeners could have heard was pre-recorded crowd noise, and me snoring.

A few quick gulps of Coca-Cola brought me back to reality. I don't know how long I dozed off, or whether I resumed play-by-play at the precise spot it was interrupted, but

CHAPTER 2: MY CAREER TAKES OFF

it was hardly a proud moment. It's bad enough for an announcer to put his listeners to sleep, but to coax himself into slumber might be grounds for dismissal. Merrill Lindsay, my manager, was difficult to please, but when I arrived for work the next day, he never once referred to the broadcast. I later thought that maybe I had put him to sleep, before I drifted into the land of nod.

Certainly a small portion of any announcer's commentary should be aimed toward intensely attentive fans who make a study of baseball's nuances. But, the announcer shouldn't do a broadcast as though he's conducting a clinic. Even while including many details, in order to give listeners a full picture of what's transpiring, it should be clear and easy to comprehend. The most important adage was: Don't ever let more than three minutes elapse without repeating the score. The famous announcer, Red Barber, kept a three minute egg timer in front of him and every time he had to flip it over…he gave the score.

The primary role of an announcer is that of a reporter and, secondarily, that of an entertainer. Let the audience enjoy the game at their preferred level. If listeners happen to acquire some baseball knowledge, consider it a bonus.

Veteran Chicago announcer Bob Elson, who did several World Series, believed silence was golden. There were times when Elson's pacing was a mite slow but many listeners preferred it that way. Bob's attributes included a resonant, golden voice and flawless enunciation. Listeners never had to wonder, "What did he say?" Additionally he was animated when the situation called for it. He didn't resort to false hype. Bob was also an accomplished interviewer. One day I discussed the art of interviewing with veteran Houston Astros' radio broadcaster, Milo Hamilton, who once worked with Elson. Milo emphatically stated: "Bob Elson was a superb interviewer because he was such an attentive listener. He let his guests talk, then responded accordingly."

Elson once hosted a Chicago radio program devoted to interviewing celebrities. One day his guest was America's very eloquent and dignified first lady, Eleanor Roosevelt. I'll never forget Bob's closing lines, "Mrs. Roosevelt, it has been our great pleasure and privilege to have you join us today at Twentieth Century Limited, and, as a memento of the occasion, I'd like to present you with a year's supply of Krank shave cream." Unruffled, Mrs. Roosevelt graciously accepted. I'm sure Franklin made good use of it.

Elson was one of the finest gentlemen I ever met in broadcasting. Early in my career, I journeyed to Chicago from Freeport with the hope of enlisting Elson's assistance in improving my job situation. Without an appointment, I searched him out on the field before a White Sox game in Comiskey Park. He was somewhat brusque, informing me he would have no time to see me until after the game.

In a sudden change of heart, he invited me to walk upstairs and accompany him to the booth. As I recall, I wasn't even keeping score but, simply observing the game, when suddenly he introduced me and brought me to the microphone to describe the third inning of a White Sox-Washington Senators game in 1951 on the Sox network. He even invited me back for additional play-by-play work later in the game. It was an educational experience from a gracious man.

3 THE ROUNDBALL MARATHON

After the 1947 baseball season ended in Decatur, I wanted to remain at WSOY. However, the station manager doubled as an announcer for University of Illinois football and basketball games, along with some high school coverage so there was no room for me. I found an opening at an FM station in Freeport, Illinois. There, I became involved not only in sports announcing but disc jockeying, newscasting, interviewing, commercial work and selling the broadcast to local sponsors. I covered two high schools' football and basketball games, an AAU basketball schedule and announced University of Wisconsin Big Ten basketball games in Madison, 70 miles away. I even broadcast a few NBA games played on a neutral court in nearby Rockford.

One basketball announcing assignment I didn't relish was doing Harlem Globetrotters' games. It was difficult to work up enthusiasm when you knew the outcome in advance.

Imaginative nicknames of Illinois high school teams always intrigued me. The Freeport Pretzels were so named because of the city's many German immigrants' fondness for that treat.

Or, how about the rivalry that pitted the Teutopolis "Wooden Shoes" against the Effingham "Flaming Hearts"? Who could ever forget the Cobden "Apple Knockers", or the Mt. Carmel "Caravan"?

For a city with the modest population of 23,000, Freeport had an impressive number of athletes who performed in great American sports events - college and professional. Don Hershberger played for Michigan in the Wolverines' historic conquest of Southern California in the 1948 Rose Bowl. Emil Yde pitched for the Pittsburgh Pirates in the 1927 World Series against the Yankees. Deacon Davis and Carl Cain were regulars on the Iowa Hawkeyes basketball team that advanced to the Final Four in 1955. The following year, Cain captained the Hawkeyes in the national championship game against the storied San Francisco Dons and their stars, Bill Russell and K.C. Jones.

More recently, Freeporter Preston Pearson played for the Dallas Cowboys in the Super Bowl. And, not to be forgotten, college basketball coaching legend Adolph "the Baron" Rupp went directly from Freeport High School to his career at Kentucky.

I met and interviewed many sports celebrities who came to Freeport, including Red Grange, the immortal "Galloping Ghost," who once scored four touchdowns in the first quarter leading Illinois to an overwhelming victory over Michigan. I became acquainted with Harry Stuhldreher, quarterback of the fabled Four Horsemen of Notre Dame under Knute Rockne. "Moon" Mullins, a halfback under Rockne,

CHAPTER 3: THE ROUNDBALL MARATHON 21

joined me for a studio interview, as did Wally Fromhart, an Irish quarterback who played for another "Horseman," fullback Elmer Layden. It was in Freeport that I visited with Billy Barrett, a starting halfback on one of Frank Leahy's national championship teams. Ivy Williamson, coach of Wisconsin's 1952 Rose Bowl team, was another whom I met in Freeport. Famous miler Glen Cunningham joined me for a lengthy studio interview in Freeport. Perhaps Freeport should have erected a mini-Golden Dome.

I, however, did experience some anxious moments in Freeport. In March 1948, immediately following a hectic and very busy basketball season, station manager, Roland Fenz informed me my services were no longer required. I was stunned. I honestly felt I had done an outstanding job and had gotten excellent listener response. I had been hired primarily as a sports announcer, but also filled in competently as newscaster and daily disc jockey.

I confronted station owner and newspaper publisher Donald Breed, the man who hired me, "What in hell is going on?" I asked. It was a good thing that I spoke up. Instead of my being fired; Fenz got the ax.

While in Freeport, I dated and fell in love with a beautiful girl named Ottie Secker. When I proposed in December, 1950, I promised I would deliver a ring the following evening. After making my exquisite purchase the next day, I carefully placed the ring in the glove compartment of my trusty 15-year-old Studebaker. About an hour and a half went by the next evening at Ottie's home before I suddenly sensed something was missing. It was the ring…still in the car. Ottie later told me she experienced some anxious moments before

I produced the precious gem. So much for my so-called steel trap memory. That winter I announced so many basketball games that a significant amount of our courtship was conducted at courtside, where Ottie turned out to be a most proficient statistician.

Once, station WFJS conducted a survey of its listening audience and invited suggestions about how the station could improve its programming. One listener, and supposed friend, Clark Reiser, wrote in with a pointed suggestion, "Get a new sports announcer." Some friend.

Illinois high school football was hardly my favorite assignment, due to sub-par working conditions. Lights were uniformly bad, numbers were frequently small and difficult to read, and at least two places, Joliet and Elgin, had no press box facilities. I broadcast from the sidelines, the worst possible vantage point. I was often screened from the ball carrier and had constant difficulty determining on what yard line the ball was located. In punting situations, I would literally jog down field to find out where the punt returner fielded the ball. At other times, as cold rain fell, accompanied by a raw, brutal wind, spotters deserted me at halftime and I was left to fend for myself.

Freeport was accustomed to playing Friday night double headers. I announced both games. I was exposed to the cruel elements for five hours as mid-November temperatures plummeted to ten degrees; a teeth-chattering experience. No wonder I so enthusiastically welcomed the start of basketball season.

Believe it or not, while in Freeport, I would routinely broadcast in excess of 100 basketball games per season. Once,

CHAPTER 3: THE ROUNDBALL MARATHON

in Champaign, Illinois, I announced six games in a single day during the state tournament, including several pre-game and halftime interviews along with post-game wrap-ups. Illinois had only one classification, regardless of the schools' enrollment.

There were 16 games in four days. They called it the "Sweet Sixteen," comprised of fifteen sectional champions and the Chicago City Kingpins.

One aspect of broadcasting six games in one day: you'd better have memorized names and numbers. The art of speaking swiftly and fluently was useless if you couldn't handle the rapid memory work required to announce several games in one day. Spotters were fairly useless for a basketball broadcaster. The game moves too quickly for the announcer to take his eye off the court and glance at the score book. I normally had two assistants with me during broadcasts. They functioned only as statisticians.

Because of the limited seating capacity of George Huff Gymnasium (just under 7,000) the tournament became a scalper's paradise and, for a high school event, the amount of gambling was astounding.

Illinois high school basketball put severe pressure on players who survived deep into post-season. Freeport's record was 31-2 in their championship season. Competing through regional and sectional tourneys to qualify for the "Sweet Sixteen" state tournament, they played NINE post season games in a span of three weeks. To make the grind even more difficult, they were forced to play both semi-finals and finals ON THE SAME DAY. This was in an era during which even major collegiate basketball teams were restricted to 25 games.

Freeport went berserk when its beloved "Pretzels" captured the grand prize. Exactly a century earlier, Abraham Lincoln bested Stephen Douglas in a debate at Taylor Park. A statue commemorates their famous oratorical duel. A waggish, irreverent sportswriter observed, "Between the debate and the Pretzels' ascent to the pinnacle; this town has been out to lunch for a hundred years."

One of radio's most timeworn and moronic pranks was called "Light the Fire." It occurred when an announcer would be in the home stretch of a five-minute newscast. At that precise juncture, a co-worker would put a match to the copy at the top of the page. The announcer's task was to finish reading his material before the flames destroyed his chances of completing the newscast. They got me one time in Freeport. I didn't finish the newscast, but I didn't go up in flames either, at least not, literally.

The Freeport radio station spent so much time broadcasting sports, promoting and selling events, that they didn't devote sufficient attention to other hours of their broadcasting day and sales lagged accordingly. After I had been there more than four years, I heard that the newspaper-owned station would soon fold. I intensified my search for a sportscasting job that would provide a semblance of stability (what was I thinking?) and the chance to work in a larger market with commensurate rewards.

4 KEEP THOSE BAGS PACKED

I heard about a possible basketball announcing job in Peoria, Illinois. I sent a letter and sample recording. Based on that, station manager, Paul Enright, hired me to broadcast games of the Peoria Caterpillars' National Industrial League team.

I would do color on home games, working with Johnny O'Hara who broadcast White Sox games in the early thirties. He later did both Cardinals and Browns baseball in St. Louis, paired with legendary Gas House Gang pitcher Dizzy Dean. I had heard O'Hara when I was a nine-year-old in Chicago and eagerly looked forward to working with him in the basketball hotbed of Peoria.

O'Hara was known to not always be reliable with regard to attendance on road games. The station's plan was to have me do play-by-play on the road, and handle color while O'Hara did play-by-play during home contests. O'Hara however, wasn't receptive to the idea and proceeded to tell the station what they could do with their broadcasts. So the announcing job was all mine, play-by-play and color, home and road games alike. I never got to meet O'Hara, who remained in St. Louis.

The Peoria Caterpillars played an enormous schedule of games for a so-called 'amateur' team. The lures to attract players were high paying jobs in a major industry and the opportunity for steady advancement. Basketball was merely a stepping stone to many a lucrative company job. Not only did the "Cats" play a full schedule of National Industrial League games, they frequently opposed topflight college teams around the country to publicize the company's name. I'd wager they played as many as 75 games my first season. That included the National AAU and U.S. Olympic post season tournaments. I quickly became accustomed to riding a winner's bandwagon. In 1952 Peoria won the prestigious National AAU tourney; a weeklong event in the Mile High city that highlighted Denver's sports year.

Some of the players, Jim Loscutoff and George Yardley, eventually advanced to the NBA. Many others could have played pro basketball, but their jobs paid more and provided a more stable future than the NBA did at the time.

During that first Peoria season, 1951-52, after concentrating on high school games the year before, I found myself travelling by train, plane, and bus to places like Milwaukee, St. Paul, Houston, Denver, San Francisco, Los Angeles and many other cities. Peoria defeated Seattle University in the exciting era of the O'Brien twins, Eddie and Johnny. The travelling at times was mind-boggling. Frequently when I awakened in the morning, whether on a train or in a hotel, I couldn't immediately remember where I was. At times I felt like I was covering the Harlem Globetrotters, with a series of one-night stands.

CHAPTER 4: KEEP THOSE BAGS PACKED

One road trip lasted three weeks, something not too easy on our families back home in Peoria. My wife Ottie gave birth to our first two children, Pat and Susie, a year and a day apart during those two hectic seasons.

One of the treats asssociated with broadcasting Peoria Caterpillars' basketball was visiting with Fibber McGee and Molly, of radio and television fame. They were Peoria natives, whose real names were Jim and Marion Jordan. They rolled out the red carpet when trainer Don Leake and I visited them at their Sherman Oaks, California home. It was wintertime and Molly (Marion) urged us to go into the back yard and pluck delectable goodies from their bountiful fruit trees. I can't recall whether Don responded to her suggestion, but I know I did. The two of them gave us the grand tour of Hollywood, Beverly Hills and various landmarks, pointing out the homes of Clark Gable, Jane Russell, Groucho Marx and others. There was one problem. We were due at the airport in Inglewood to catch a flight to San Francisco, for our next game. Absent-minded Fibber (Jim), with an undeveloped sense of direction, became lost en route to the airport. He finally got his bearings so we were able to avoid missing the flight.

Molly was definitely more aggressive than Fibber. I interviewed Fibber at the National AAU Tournament in Denver at halftime of a game involving their favorite team. Obviously wanting to play a role in the interview, Molly seized the microphone from Fibber's hand and the fun began.

I had a sobering scare during my first Peoria season. After I'd been there for six weeks, WWXL was forced off the air, its doors padlocked by the Federal Communications

Commission because one of the principal owners was a doctor caught performing illegal abortions. Several staff announcers lost their jobs, as I did briefly just before our first baby was born. We had virtually no savings. Such was the exciting, glamorous world of broadcasting!

Luckily for me and my family, basketball interest was so high in Peoria that another station, WIRL, agreed to pick up the broadcasts in mid-season.

So many memories abound of that first Peoria season. Some of the players liked to test Coach Warren Womble, famed as a successful Olympic head coach, by arriving, for a seven a.m. train departure from Peoria, at precisely…6:59. One player, Wisconsin alumnus, Bob Harlow, was so impoverished, that he saved substantial sums from his meal money by wolfing down inexpensive hamburgers instead of occasionally indulging in an expensive steak. Teammates badgered him so mercilessly for his frugal ways, that every time we passed a "White Castle" or "Wimpy's" restaurant, they suggested Harlow get off the bus, for his thrifty treat.

Frequently I roomed with trainer Pat Doyle who very coherently mouthed startlingly foul language in his sleep. Many years earlier he was a Texas League baseball umpire. He got into such a heated argument with Ft. Worth outfielder Ziggy Sears that, after the game, the incensed Doyle entered Ft. Worth's locker room armed with a pistol, loudly threatening to zero in on Sears.

"Please, don't shoot, Mr. Doyle," the player reportedly begged.

Players invariably scoffed at Doyle whenever he related the story, but Pat had the last word on a trip to Houston. A

CHAPTER 4: KEEP THOSE BAGS PACKED

sportswriter ran a lengthy feature story, above which appeared the headline, "Please, don't shoot me!"

In spring, 1952, the "Cats" won the National AAU championship in Denver. The team then moved on to the U.S. Olympic tourney at New York's Madison Square Garden. We won the weeklong struggle there, beating AAU, service, and topflight college teams to capture the American Olympic crown. That gained the Caterpillars wholesale representation on the team that would represent the U.S. at the World Games in Helsinki.

In the climactic title game, Peoria defeated an NCAA championship Kansas team coached by the immortal Phog Allen and spearheaded by everybody's All-American, high scoring Clyde Lovelette. Peoria prevailed on a last second shot by Ron Bontemps after Lovelette had missed the easiest shot of his life, an uncontested lay-up.

During the U.S. Olympic classic, many teams were quartered at the Paramount Hotel in the heart of downtown Manhattan. Little more than a year earlier, gamblers and guilty players in that very hotel arranged the basketball fixes and point shavings. Money even changed hands right there at the Paramount. Possibly another location would have been a better choice, but that's not what happened, go figure.

I remember the unusual combination of names that comprised the Kansas lineup. There was Lovelette, of course, but also in the lineup were John Keller, Bill Kenney, Al and Dean Kelly and a threesome that included Hoag, Hoaglund and Heitholt. One Jayhawk player, Dean Smith, would become the North Carolina coaching icon.

For pronunciation challenges, how about a squad whose roster became available to me about a half-hour before airtime, the unforgettable Waukegan, Illinois Cyclones. These were the names of the first seven players: Pavelich, Sekulich, Sikich, Staskiewicz, Gagula, Daluga and Gugala. Try mixing those up during the rapid-fire sequence demanded of an announcer in a fast moving basketball game.

Once during a Denver Bears' baseball broadcast, I recounted that story for the KOA listening audience. Mark Holtz, my broadcast partner for five years before he became the voice of the Texas Rangers, laughed so uproariously it took him 15 minutes to regain his composure. Mark challenged me to repeat the names later in the broadcast, which I promptly did and again he went into hysterics. KOA still airs playbacks of that memorable broadcast.

Once, during a football game, I informed my listeners that Kosikowski and Klimazewski, were being replaced by Fish and Fink. Or how about the lyrical sounding Evansville, Indiana battery of Whitcher, the pitcher, and Fletcher, the catcher! A few of the more memorable.

Picking up the basketball adventure in mid-June, 1952, Peoria and Kansas, who would comprise the bulk of the U.S. Olympic team, played a series of exhibition games, first in Hutchinson, then in Peoria before the team embarked for Helsinki. I announced every one of those exhibition games in June and July in sweltering heat in non-air conditioned arenas. It was so hot in Hutchinson that some media members stripped down to their shorts in a futile attempt to stay cool. It was a vision I won't soon forget.

CHAPTER 4: KEEP THOSE BAGS PACKED

I very nearly accompanied the U.S. team to Finland. Some of the Caterpillar Tractor Company executives were in favor of sending me there to do reports and features on the basketball team, as well as interviews with more famous track and field competitors such as Emil Zatopek and Reverend Bob Richards. But the anticipated expense proved to be prohibitive.

I had another experience I'll forever remember. The Cats were battling the Houston Ada Oilers at Bradley Fieldhouse. I described a play where a Peoria defender undercut a 215-pound Houston forward, Royce Ray, breaking down the lane toward the baseline. Ray was knocked off balance and flew through the air, landing right in the lap of a spectator seated in the first row of seats just beyond the end line. Until that moment I was unaware of the spectator's identity. To my great surprise I discovered it was my wife, eight months pregnant!

I had no idea she was in the building. She had received a last minute ride to the game from a neighbor. Fortunately, Ottie survived the collision unharmed. Later, I jokingly commented, "Thank God I married an Amazon."

At the time we lived in Peoria, the city had an impressive array of broadcasters. Working down the street from me, describing Bradley basketball and Big Ten football, was Chick Hearn. It seems Chick had been the voice of the Los Angeles Lakers forever, before he passed away in the summer of 2002.

Also on the scene, in direct competition with Hearn, was Jack Quinn, veteran Bradley play-by-play man who later became Jack Quinlan, the long-time radio voice of the Chicago Cubs and Bears. Quinlan also described the 1960 World Series during which Bill Mazeroski belted his famous Series-ending homer.

Bill King, the current Oakland Athletics broadcaster, was another Peoria announcer. In earlier years Jack Brickhouse, and later Vince Lloyd, left Peoria to announce big league baseball and other sports in Chicago. Long after I left Peoria, Mark Holtz was there, broadcasting Bradley basketball and Big Ten football before we teamed up for five years of Denver Bears' baseball broadcasts.

There was one major void in Peoria. While no city in the nation could have kept an announcer busier during basketball season, there was no minor league baseball at that time. My station, WIRL, affiliated with both ABC and the Mutual Networks, couldn't clear time on weekdays or weeknights to carry live broadcasts of St. Louis Cardinal games, which they did air on weekends. Because Peoria was a Cardinal hotbed, I thought why not do condensed re-creations of St. Louis games that could be aired after WIRL's evening network commitments were fulfilled? I would condense Cardinals' games to about 45 minutes. The program, I correctly figured, would elicit enthusiastic response in sports-happy Peoria.

I wrote Cardinals' owner Fred Saigh, requesting permission. Not only did he graciously grant me permission, but he didn't propose charging the station a single penny for the rights. Saigh even invited me to visit with him during my next trip to St. Louis.

Because no Peoria area station carried Cardinals' games except on Saturdays and Sundays, I was concerned about

CHAPTER 4: KEEP THOSE BAGS PACKED

how I would receive play-by-play reports, batter by batter, so I could later do my condensed re-creation. A station in Bloomington, Illinois, 60 miles from Peoria, carried live broadcasts of all St. Louis games. The signal was accompanied by annoying static, but I was still able to follow the broadcast and keep score, thanks to Harry Caray's description and Gus Mancuso's expert analysis.

Just how does a broadcaster compress a 2 1/2-hour game into 45 minutes? You cut down on elapsed time between pitches. Unless a batter walks or strikes out, you seldom let the count run to its maximum.

I also had a nightly 15-minute sportscast preceding my re-creations, which was the perfect lead-in. The sponsor was Grisedieck Brothers Beer, Caray's Cardinal network sponsor, but, "This Grisedieck's for you," probably would have never caught on.

5 SHOW ME THE MONEY?

Having proven my worth to WIRL, I twice asked for a raise. Station manager, Tom Gavin assured me I'd be properly compensated; however, several weeks went by with no raise. Meanwhile, I discovered a new station, WTVH, would soon go on the air. I approached Peoria Caterpillar Company executives and informed them of my unsuccessful attempts to secure a needed pay raise. I asked them if they would object to my seeking another outlet for upcoming basketball broadcasts, and they said they wouldn't. I approached WTVH management and found they'd be thrilled to secure rights to broadcast Caterpillars' games and quickly agreed to my salary request. I then went back to Caterpillar executives to inform them of WTVH's interest, whereupon the deal was consummated.

    WIRL manager Gavin was furious. I reminded him that I had twice requested a well-deserved pay raise, and had tired of his stalling. He had left me no alternative. For their refusal to treat me fairly, WIRL had lost the rights to the prestigious and lucrative tie-in with Peoria's number one industry.

During my two seasons with what seemed like the Caterpillars' traveling basketball circus and with Peoria still without professional baseball, I called on radio stations in cities that had minor league baseball teams.

I paid a visit to KTHT in Houston, the outlet for the Buffalos' Texas League broadcasts. I was able without appointment to get an interview with station manager Bill Bennett. He offered me nothing tangible, but I knew he would keep my recording on file. This was in mid-January, 1953, close to the time my wife, Ottie, would give birth to our second child, Susie, back in Freeport where her parents lived.

Finally, the regular season ended and I prepared for another trip to Denver to broadcast the National AAU basketball tourney. The Caterpillars would be defending the championship they had won the previous March.

Shortly before I was to depart by train for the Mile High City, Bill Bennett in Houston called. KTHT was about to add an announcer to their broadcast team and they had chosen my tape. Was I still interested? Was he kidding? "When can you come to Houston?" he asked. "Would yesterday be too soon?" I asked.

It was early March and I was all packed for Denver. I told Bennett I would be able to leave for Houston in two weeks. That seemed to be plenty of time since Houston's baseball season wouldn't start until early April. Bennett, however, told me it was urgent I get to Houston by mid-March. When I explained the situation to WTVH management in Peoria, they reacted with total understanding. Not only did they graciously release me from my commitment to broad-

CHAPTER 5: SHOW ME THE MONEY?

cast the National AAU tourney in Denver, but, they presented me with an expensive new suit as a going away present.

Leaving behind a wife and two tiny children – one a newborn, I set out for Houston. Upon my arrival, Bennett casually inquired where I was staying. He then suggested, "Why don't you check out of your motel and move to Roy Hofheinz' suite. He won't be occupying it for awhile."

Hofheinz' quarters were indeed luxurious. I stayed there for nearly a month while searching for a house to rent so Ottie and the two babies could join me. The Hofheinz I refer to was mayor of Houston at the time and owner of KTHT. He would later conceive the idea of the Astrodome (the Eighth Wonder of the World) and become owner of the Houston Colt 45s when they became a National League expansion club.

Bennett told me why and how my new job opened up. Between the time of my January visit and audition at KTHT, Cardinals' owner Fred Saigh (yes, the same man who had so kindly granted me permission to re-create St. Louis games the previous summer) was sentenced to a federal penitentiary for income tax evasion. He was thus forced to sell his beloved baseball team.

The new principal owner was August A. Busch, Jr., who also owned Anheuser-Busch, brewers of Budweiser. Budweiser soon contracted to sponsor baseball broadcasts in virtually every city in the Cardinals' wide ranging farm system, places like Rochester, Columbus, Fresno, Winston-Salem, and Houston, the largest city in the St. Louis chain. Budweiser advertising executives wanted to enhance the Houston broadcasts with a second announcer, paving the way for me to work with Loel Passe. He later became the first voice of the major league Colts (later Astros).

How strange those early days of radio were. I latched onto the Peoria job because the previous Caterpillars' announcer had a personal problem. Then I landed the Houston assignment because the St. Louis Cardinals' owner was sent to prison.

Shortly after my arrival, I traveled with Passe to St. Louis. For three days we toured the Anheuser-Busch brewery. We sampled their famous product, the better to talk about when we'd do the live Budweiser commercials.

I've had many broadcast partners but none more different than Loel Passe, a native of Birmingham, Alabama. He injected expressions into a broadcast I had never heard before, nor since. If he wanted a Houston pitcher to strike out an opposing batter, he would implore the hurler to, "Breeze him one time." He was just like a fan in the stands. If the pitcher obliged, Loel would typically respond very enthusiastically, "Now you chuckin', boy. Hot ziggety dog and good ole sassafras tea."

My first broadcasts with Loel Passe were exhibition games that involved trips to cities such as Galveston, Beaumont and Port Arthur. It wasn't particularly easy working with Loel those early days. He didn't adjust readily to working with a partner. The business of sports announcing is so competitive it can lead to paranoia at times, even if wholly unwarranted. The season was two months old when Bill Bennett summoned me to his office and told me, "The broadcasts sound great." He casually added, "Loel is finally convinced you're not after his job."

CHAPTER 5: SHOW ME THE MONEY?

During the 1953 season, "Gussie" Busch and his entourage paid a visit to Houston. Loel and I received explicit orders from D'Arcy Advertising representatives to accompany Busch and his party wherever they went after the games, no matter how deep into the night their celebrations lasted. It seemed ridiculous to me how our entire group kowtowed to the notorious beer baron.

I remember one particular incident. Busch, new to baseball was soliciting opinions of how the 1953 Cardinals could best improve. General manager, Bill Walsingham, unafraid to speak up, voiced the view that St. Louis would remain mediocre until they shored up the left side of their infield. Walsingham contended that third baseman Ray Jablonski and shortstop Solly Hemus were "killing them" defensively. Busch, quickly took issue, whereupon Walsingham, an outstanding veteran baseball executive, startled everyone at the table by rising to his feet, and exclaiming, "Gentlemen, see you later." With that he walked out on his stunned employer. Strangely, the Cardinals had a new general manager by the following season.

The Texas League had a longer schedule of games than the majors. We played 168 games to their 154. Summer heat, in south Texas, was often overwhelming, but I don't ever recall fans complaining. Houston and San Antonio played an afternoon double header on July 4, 1954, a blistering hot day accompanied by high humidity that left you drenched if you were simply sitting still. Did that induce fans to seek cooler pursuits? No way!

Not only was old Buff Stadium filled to capacity, but ropes were stretched across the outfield warning tracks, foul line to foul line, to accommodate the overflow throng spilling onto the field to watch. I don't recall any fans suffering from sunstroke or heat prostration, but then again they were so packed together, who'd have known if they passed out.

I've long had an antipathy for baseball played indoors on synthetic turf. I don't like indoor football either, having broadcast it in both Houston's Astrodome and New Orleans' Superdome. But, particularly in baseball, the game is so drastically altered. In both sports the chance of injuries is sharply increased. Astroturf came into being when Hofheinz and his engineering experts made the belated discovery that natural grass wouldn't grow in the Astrodome because of lack of sunlight.

Personally, I liked Hofheinz, a fine man to work for. He was often called "Judge" because at age 24 he was a practicing Harris County jurist, then, later became Lyndon Johnson's campaign manager in LBJ's successful run for the United States Senate.

Houston had an outfielder in 1954 who hit over .500 as a spring training sensation. His name was Paul Donovan and he seemed a sure-fire bet to achieve big league stardom. But as the season began he appeared to be undergoing a bewildering personality change. He became not standoffish, but painfully quiet. I noticed the alarming change when I would occasionally drive him to his hotel following a game. His performance suffered and Houston sent him packing, never to fulfill the brilliant promise. My guess is Donovan was suffering from a deep depression despite his obvious talents.

CHAPTER 5: SHOW ME THE MONEY?

Harry Caray called me one day from Houston's Shamrock Hotel. He was there to broadcast a basketball game between the Houston University Cougars and the St. Louis University Billikens. Harry was a monumental figure in the world of sports broadcasting, yet his lack of even the most basic preparation astounded me. Rosters with players' numbers, press guides and the other printed matter were available in abundance to help writers and broadcasters in their preparations. Yet about 45 minutes before air time Harry jovially asked me to give him the names of "some of your players."

He began to mark crooked lines on a blank legal pad, separating players' names from columns for baskets, free throws, personal fouls, etc. Keep in mind that I hadn't followed the Houston team that closely. I was much more familiar with the Rice Owls in the prestigious Southwest Conference. Harry did halftime interviews with Houstonians Johnny Keane and Solly Hemus. Despite an obvious lack of preparation, Harry was his usual entertaining and effervescent self.

That was the day of a historic "straight up" trade in which the New York Giants swapped the legendary Bobby Thomson to Milwaukee in exchange for budding young pitcher Johnny Antonelli. Thomson was on a sharp decline and that very year Antonelli emerged as the pitching hero of the 1954 Giants' World Series sweep over favored Cleveland.

That same year the Giants played an exhibition game against Cactus League rival Cleveland in Houston. I stood alongside Leo Durocher before the game. He was difficult to interview because he talked non-stop. The Houston groundskeeper visibly ruffled Leo's feathers when he inquired, "How ya doin, Mister Day?" You may recall that Leo was once married to glamorous movie actress Larraine Day. It was one of the few times I ever saw Leo speechless.

In Houston, not only did we broadcast all 168 regular season games, but in 1954 the team played 21-post season games. There were two rounds of Texas League Shaughnessy playoffs, that each went the maximum seven games. Then came the Dixie Series, the World Series of the South, which also was extended through seven games.

We made two trips to Atlanta in one week with three games sandwiched between in Houston. Buffs' manager Dixie Walker, who replaced fired Al Hollingsworth during the 1953 season, had a talented array of ball players in 1954. The ex-Brooklyn Dodger hero skippered several players who achieved major league success, including World Series glory. Those players were Ken Boyer, Luis Arroyo, Don Blasingame, Hal Smith, Willard Schmidt and a baffling knuckleballer named Bobby Tiefenauer.

The 1954 Dixie Series was memorable in many respects. It pitted the Texas League playoff champs against the Southern Association's playoff kingpins. It was Houston vs. Atlanta in the "World Series of the South." Two Brooklyn Dodger teammates on the 1941 National League champions were rival managers, Dixie Walker and Whitlow Wyatt, both Georgians. The Dixie Series attracted nearly 100,000 fans. Over 18,000 poured into old Ponce de Leon Park, with its three decks of advertising signs, for the opener. They rose

CHAPTER 5: SHOW ME THE MONEY?   43

to their feet in unison to sing "Dixie" before each Atlanta game.

The Atlanta Crackers boasted such standouts as Chuck Tanner, Frank Torre, Dick Donovan and Don McMahon. Houston seized a 3 to 1 lead, then dropped the final three games. Walker was so incensed he refused to board the airplane that carried the Buffs back to Houston after the final game. I never again saw Dixie Walker, but got to know his brother Harry well when he managed Jacksonville, Florida in the International League.

Near the end of my second Houston season, the Cardinals announced they were moving one of their Triple A franchises, the Columbus Redbirds, to Omaha. That was the same year, 1955, that Kansas City became a major league city, inheriting the financially strapped Philadelphia Athletics. Harry Renfro, the D'Arcy Advertising Company executive in charge of hiring broadcasters for the entire St. Louis Cardinals' empire, asked me if I'd be interested in moving to Omaha to take over as the Triple A announcer. I was only doing a couple of innings per game in Houston, along with color, a pregame interview and a post-game program.

An important consideration in making my decision, was an acute personality clash I had with Houston General Manager Art Routzong. To this very day I don't know what caused our problems, but Routzong had always acted distant and sometimes downright hostile toward me.

When it was announced I would be leaving Houston, baseball people like Eddie Dyer and Gus Mancuso were flabbergasted. Dyer, who managed the Cardinals for five seasons and directed them to a World Series triumph in 1946, would sometimes call me at home to solicit my opinions of certain prospects.

Shortly after I left Houston, Routzong mailed me my Texas League championship ring. Years later I ran into him on a few occasions. He even gave me a personal tour of the Astrodome. After he moved to St. Louis as the Cardinals' assistant general manager under Bing Devine, he invited me to his home and I accepted. I'll never know why the turnaround, but I welcomed his change of heart.

6 ANOTHER MOVE—
SAME OLD CHALLENGE

The chance to do Triple A baseball, along with Creighton University basketball, Omaha University basketball and football, and a heavy slate of high school football and basketball made Omaha extremely attractive. In October 1954, we packed up…again, and moved to Omaha at our own expense.

I remember broadcasting a high school basketball game at Boys Town, just outside Omaha. During my first broadcast one of my two "Boys Town" statisticians made a minor error. The other young man reached across in front of me and belted his partner. Boys Town was populated by some tough kids. I was just glad I hadn't made any broadcasting mistakes.

Heightening my interest in broadcasting Creighton basketball games was the dazzling performance consistently delivered by a Blue Jays' forward named Bob Gibson, who later played for the Harlem Globetrotters. Yes, It's the same Bob Gibson who would later become a Cardinals' pitching immortal.

Curiously, even though I was very familiar with Bob Gibson the basketball player, I saw him pitch only once. It was game four of the 1968 World Series against 31 game winner Dennis McLain. During a lengthy rain delay I ventured into the Cardinals' clubhouse to record interviews with Manager Red Schoendienst, Stan Musial, Tim McCarver and Mike Shannon. During the seemingly interminable delay, I spotted Gibson, relaxing on the trainer's table, indulging himself in "Nutty Buddy" ice cream cones. So much for World Series pressure.

I specifically recall the kindness of two Cardinals in that World Series, outfielders Lou Brock and the controversial and oft-times bad tempered Roger Maris. While interviewing Brock before game five, I had problems with my recorder. Lou, the consummate gentleman, waited patiently. He refused to be interviewed by others clamoring for his attention and cordially resumed the interview as though there had been no interruption. That same day, he became the Series "goat" when he neglected to slide on a close play and was cut down at home plate. Had he scored, St. Louis would have remained world champions.

After I interviewed Maris, the man who shattered Babe Ruth's single season home run record, he graciously suggested I use his locker space to conduct additional interviews. I never saw Maris again…but I'll always remember him fondly.

Many famous sports personalities came to Omaha. I once had breakfast with Jackie Robinson, still a Dodger player who would perform two more seasons in Brooklyn. While interviewing him, I discovered his electrifying personality came right through the microphone.

Rocky Marciano, reigning heavy weight boxing champ, invited me to interview him in his hotel room. I gladly accepted, and found him to be one of the most likeable and gracious athletes I ever met.

Fabled Olympic sprinter Jesse Owens agreed to join me in the KOIL studios for an interview. Arriving late, he offered a unique excuse. He'd neglected to pack an extra pair of trousers for the trip, so he had to send out his only pants for pressing. Owens was a delight, a professional broadcaster, who hosted his own radio program in Chicago.

Ice skating star Barbara Ann Scott joined me in the studio, accompanied by two very lively poodles, and that same day, I did a telephone interview with Harry Caray, during which he congratulated me upon becoming a Triple A baseball announcer.

Cardinal front office executives came to Omaha when Triple A baseball became official there. I was invited to join the party on August Busch's luxurious train. And I do mean luxurious with every conceivable trapping. While on the train I taped interviews with Busch and his feisty, swaggering manager, Eddie Stanky.

I was thoroughly enjoying the world of broadcasting when KOIL manager Don Burden suddenly summoned me to a meeting. Burden, who could be extremely curt and downright insulting to employees, had always treated me extremely well. He hired me for a generous base salary with no promises of additional fees or bonuses for various assignments. Despite this, he paid me a handsome fee for every game I broadcast, high school or college.

When I reached Burden's office, he was wearing a somber expression. Without mincing words, he informed me I wouldn't be broadcasting baseball in Omaha.

What? That was the very assignment that had lured me to Nebraska. Announcing football and basketball merely sweetened the pot.

I still hadn't recovered from the overwhelming shock of such horrible news when Burden informed me that Don Hill, announcer of Columbus Red Birds' games, would be moving to Omaha along with the transplanted franchise. Harry Renfro of D'Arcy Advertising hadn't been the final voice, after all, in selecting the Omaha announcer. Although I had met "Gussie" Busch and interviewed him, I obviously didn't know him as well as Hill did.

My world in Omaha collapsed. I received the startling news on our oldest son Pat's third birthday, and to make the day still worse, he'd fallen down a flight of stairs. Fortunately, he escaped serious injury.

It was imperative that I pursue other possibilities. It was late January and most teams in the high minors already had chosen their announcers. I remembered that Fort Worth Cats' general manager Spencer Harris told me to contact him if ever I became interested in moving to that North Texas city. He had heard my play-by-play and liked it. I called Harris, only to find out he had recently hired a broadcaster from Ogden, Utah. Spencer added that on a recent trip to Oklahoma City he discovered general manager Jimmy Humphries hadn't yet decided on an announcer. I promptly called Humphries, only to find he had just hired someone.

While this personal drama was unfolding, the Cardinals' Busch and his entourage came to Omaha. They were honored at a huge banquet celebrating Omaha's ascent to Triple A baseball. At one point the entire assemblage rose in

CHAPTER 6: ANOTHER MOVE... 49

unison to cheer the St. Louis bigwigs. I remained glued to my seat, the only person in the room who didn't participate in the noisy ovation. Call me a poor sport, but I was still seething over what I considered to be a rank injustice.

I deliberately created a scene afterward when I approached Cardinals' General Manager Dick Meyer, demanding, "What happened to my broadcasting deal here?"

Meyer appeared to be taken aback, at which point another Cardinals' official, Walter Shannon, intervened and tried to placate me, telling me he would write me a letter about what happened. He never kept his promise.

At that moment when I confronted Meyer, I despised the St. Louis Cardinals' organization and their overwhelming power and control. In effect, they made a complete mockery of our expensive move to Omaha. Regretfully, I didn't have the protection of a written contract. At that level of radio in those days, contracts weren't widespread.

I was in an obvious predicament but determined to exhaust every effort to remain a baseball broadcaster. I had difficulty controlling my anger over a development that I considered to be grossly unfair, but I realized I needed to move on. Burden, a native of Idaho Falls and familiar with Salt Lake City and Ogden markets, called an Ogden radio station and discovered they were indeed seeking a replacement for their broadcaster who had departed for...Fort Worth.

Small world!

7 THE ROLLER COASTER— PLUNGES DOWNWARD

In the continuing game of musical chairs, I contacted Cecil Heftel in Ogden. He offered me the job of announcing Ogden's games in the Class C Pioneer League. Yes, CLASS C.

I'd left Double A games in Houston, graduating to Triple A baseball in Omaha. Now I was plummeting to a lower classification than Decatur, where I had begun my radio career eight years before. With two small children, we had precious little money in the bank. We moved to Ogden…again, at our own expense.

After we found out we would be moving soon, we quickly swung into action to collect our newcomer's gifts. As an advertising vehicle, Omaha businessmen presented some valuable gifts to newcomers. The Blackstone Hotel, for example, presented new arrivals with certificates for a sumptuous dinner for two. We managed to collect everything we had coming before departing for Ogden, Utah.

When I arrived in Ogden, I began work immediately at station KALL in Salt Lake City. I was loaned to KALL by KLO of Ogden to broadcast two state high school basketball tournaments in successive weeks, one in Salt Lake City and the other at Brigham Young University in Provo.

I was in Salt Lake City for a pre-season banquet when Mal Wyman, KALL's baseball announcer, passed along some disturbing news. The Cincinnati Reds, Ogden's parent club, were seriously contemplating abandoning the Ogden franchise at season's end because of dwindling attendance.

Two moves in seemingly rapid-fire sequence, Houston to Omaha, then less than six months later, Omaha to Ogden, had decimated our savings. Wyman's bombshell was almost more than we could absorb.

Difficult as it was, I had to cast aside the depressing thoughts concerning my future, in order to concentrate on preparing for Ogden's opening game in Salt Lake City. The Pioneer League was a far cry from where I had been broadcasting little more than six months previously. I missed Houston with its large Texas League crowds, and Atlanta, where huge throngs turned out for the always exciting Dixie Series.

Still, it was positively exhilarating to be broadcasting baseball again, no matter the surroundings. Two seasons earlier, Ogden had produced the great Frank Robinson. Ogden had a catcher in 1955, power hitting Jesse Gonder, who ultimately played with Casey Stengel's lovably inept New York Mets, then with the Yankees. Ogden's first baseman Karl Kuehl, just out of the high school in Downey, California, later succeeded Dick Williams as the Montreal Expos' manager.

Fairly early it became obvious that Ogden would finish in the Pioneer League basement, thanks to inadequate pitching and John Affleck Park. The Ogden Reds home field was positioned so that in the early twilight innings of night games, the sun literally shone in the hitters' eyes. Home plate should have been where center field was located. To make things even worse, those were pre-batting-helmet days.

I also did a lot of studio commercial work at KLO, along with occasional disc jockeying. I was assigned to do interviews in the Ogden training camp of Gene Fullmer, preparing for one of his many middleweight championship bouts. Outside the ring, I found Fullmer had a kind, almost gentle disposition.

Studio interviews were a part of my life in Ogden. This was when famous sports figures, past and present, would happily come to the station to be interviewed. One memorable visitor was boxer, Max Baer, who in the mid-thirties, won boxing's heavyweight crown by administering a punishing beating to Italian champion Primo Carnera. He was a powerful, but clumsy and slow-moving giant who provided an easy target for Baer's murderous assaults. Baer greeted me with a playful while still stinging jolt to the ribs, which I neglected to sidestep. I'm sure he wondered why I conducted the interview doubled over.

Jimmy Braddock was another visitor and a very willing interview guest. He had wrested the heavyweight crown from Baer. Max had a world of talent but seldom took training seriously. Braddock lost his first and only defense of the title to a rising young boxer with a knockout wallop, the legendary "Brown Bomber", Joe Louis.

Prominent golf pro, Julius Boros also came to see me. Doing these interviews was always a joy. I began to develop a special kinship with many of the people I interviewed.

As the 1955 Pioneer League season approached the home stretch, rumors surfaced that Ogden might very well lose its baseball franchise. One day while doing a live broadcast from the ballpark, the studio announcer was slow coming out of his program, so I was forced to go on the air several minutes late. I quickly informed my listeners that the game was already in progress. I gave starting lineups then, batter by batter, I recreated what had already occurred. Station manager, Cecil Heftel, was in the booth and bluntly told me I had used poor judgement, that I should have faked the early action as though the game was just starting when I went on the air. This would have been deceiving to the listeners and would have destroyed my credibility.

For example, if I was describing a routine ground ball to the second baseman as though it was just happening, and the actual batter in the game was walloping a three-run homer, prompting a loud roar from the crowd, the listeners would surely be wondering, "What the hell is going on?" Obviously, these possibilities had never occurred to Cecil, whom I probably should have promptly ejected from the booth. The repercussions, however, would have been severe.

I had still another serious run-in with Heftel. About midway through the disastrous season, the Ogden team's Board of Directors was pressuring Cincinnati to fire manager, Jim Crandall. I attended a meeting and heard sharp criticisms of Crandall. One of the more vociferous critics was sports columnist Al Warden, long an icon in that area. While Warden was verbally tearing Crandall apart, I became irate. I loudly interrupted Al and demanded to know how he felt qualified to criticize Crandall when he, Warden, had seldom attended games for a period of several weeks.

Heftel promptly took me to task for publicly criticizing Warden. I should have informed Cecil I was unaware that freedom of speech was no longer permitted. What complicated the situation was the fact that I genuinely liked Al Warden.

CHAPTER 7: ROLLER COASTER... 55

When I first came to Ogden, he wrote a wonderful column about me, complimenting me on my play-by-play work, particularly my description of the Utah high school basketball tournaments. Still, I could not let his strong criticism of Crandall go unchallenged. I thought Jim was doing a competent job of running the ball club considering the team's woeful pitching. The Reds, complied and dismissed Crandall in favor of former New York Giants outfielder, Red Treadway.

As the season drew to a close, Cincinnati sent farm director, Bill McKechnie Jr. to Ogden to appraise the situation. McKechnie's father, "Deacon Bill," managed the Pirates and Cardinals to pennants and twice took Cincinnati into the World Series. I visited with McKechnie, who joined me on my broadcasts and cordially invited me to breakfast on the day he departed for Cincinnati. We went to breakfast, had a pleasant conversation and he left. I never saw him again.

Late in the season, Cincinnati formally announced it would be moving its Pioneer League franchise to Butte, Montana. For this beleaguered broadcaster, Butte seemed a continent away from Ogden. I shuddered and shivered to think of a move to the frigid climes of faraway Butte.

Mal Wyman's pre-season foretelling of doom had indeed come to pass. Cynic that I had become, I even wondered whether Heftel knew that baseball would be leaving Ogden at season's end, before he imported me from Omaha. No one forced me to become a sports announcer; you take your chances and battle hard to remain in the business.

I felt I had been given a special talent and was determined to keep using it. I was blessed with a wife who was willing to participate in the adventure and all the heartaches. She was always ready to move, even with small children, in order that I could continue to pursue my career. What toll did the constant changing of jobs, the expensive moves, the uprooting, the relentless insecurity and the very real hardships created, take on my wife, Ottie? She suffered two nervous breakdowns.

Just one day before the 1955 Pioneer League season ended on Labor Day, I received a badly needed stroke of good fortune. I happened upon a message sent by Eddie Kime, the Pocatello announcer. Eddie's message stated that after the season ended he would be permanently leaving station KWIK in Pocatello to return to his home in St. Louis. I was desperate for employment. My time was running out in Ogden. I contacted KWIK station manager, John Taylor, told him about my situation in Ogden, and relayed to him my strong interest in joining his station. Taylor invited me for an interview.

After meeting with him, I was hired to join the staff of KWIK and jumped into re-creating Pocatello's Pioneer League playoff games. Our Ogden landlord was most accommodating in releasing us from the remainder of our lease. Even better, Cecil Heftel paid for our move to Idaho. We had acquired a minimal amount of furniture so the cost of the move was a startling, $135.

During our season in Ogden, I had enjoyed the friendship of Frank Lucchesi, who doubled as Pocatello center fielder and manager. Lucchesi liked my work and talked about me to John Taylor. So, in a very real way, a baseball manager helped open the door for me to land a radio job when I needed it most. It has frequently been said that media people have an almost adversarial relationship with baseball players, witness Billy Martin vs. the New York press. But men in baseball uniforms have often been among my prime boosters. They realize I have a keen interest in them and their game. Lucchesi went on to manage the Philadelphia Phillies, Texas Rangers and, on an interim basis, the Chicago Cubs.

My Pocatello experience wasn't confined to sports. I was also an everyday disc jockey, a newscaster and, even though I didn't possess an engineering license, I operated the control board during my three or four hour stints. I even learned to activate all station equipment before I would sign on in the morning. I was also required to line up many of my sponsors for play-by-play broadcasts.

I traveled with Idaho State College teams, along with going on the road to do high school games, it was an expensive proposition for a 250-watt station in a small market. Overhead costs could become staggering, not just my road expenses, but expensive telephone line charges when originating broadcasts from eleven states.

My hours were frequently astounding. An example: One day I signed on the station, arriving at about 4:45 a.m. to do early news and weather reports along with a three-hour disc jockey shift. Then came a trip to the airport for a flight to Spokane, Washington to broadcast an Idaho State/Gonzaga University game. I was my own engineer and that meant arriving at the scene long before game time to locate telephone lines, hook up equipment and do a routine check to make sure I was getting back to the KWIK control room in Pocatello.

I did some broadcasts on no sleep whatsoever. I once boarded a Greyhound bus in early afternoon in Pocatello and at approximately noon the next day, I arrived in San Francisco. I was there to announce an NCAA tournament game between

Idaho State and the defending national champions, the University of California Golden Bears. Cal had won the title the previous March by defeating West Virginia, led by Jerry West.

Once in town I headed immediately for the University of San Francisco Field house, which would be the site of the opening-round game.

With no sleep, and desperately trying to stay awake and alert while doing play-by-play, I had only one solution. I just drank coffee and Coke throughout the game. People later told me they enjoyed the broadcast, but that there were times I talked a little too fast. I had done many a broadcast working alone, without an announcing sidekick, or engineer.

When the equipment malfunctioned, it becomes an impossible task trying to get it operating again, while keeping track of the game. The reality was that many stations didn't have enough money to make sports broadcasts more than a one-man show. A friend once bluntly described what it meant to work in a small market such as Pocatello, "It's like shoveling sand with a pitchfork."

Compounding the situation, financial rewards in small market radio were depressingly low. Sponsors didn't pay substantial sums for exposure to a limited number of people. Advertising experts never lost sight of one of their favorite measuring sticks, cost per thousand.

I went through a lengthy period in Pocatello when the station's financial situation was so shaky that paychecks would frequently bounce. I would be on the road announcing an Idaho State football or basketball game while my wife headed for the bank planning to cash my paycheck, only to discover there weren't sufficient funds in the KWIK account.

CHAPTER 7: ROLLER COASTER...

I broadcast a football game in Pocatello sitting in a junior high school classroom looking out windows onto the playing field below, but there was one major distraction - in the classroom, a girls' volleyball game was being played, to the accompaniment of loud music. Every once in a while a stray volleyball would hit me on the head, causing an interesting pause in my play calling.

You might wonder why I remained in Pocatello for over six years. After all, I had proven myself in larger markets such as Peoria, Houston, and Omaha. Why didn't I move back up the ladder? I just couldn't seem to land a break.

I once sent a play-by-play tape, letter, and resume to Rosy Ryan, the general manager of the Phoenix Giants' Pacific Coast League ball club. The package came back unopened and readdressed to me, conclusive proof of Ryan's total lack of interest. The struggle to survive often seemed daunting. I was growing steadily more cynical. It didn't help that three changes of ownership, SIX changes of station managers and a constantly revolving door of other personnel occurred during my years in Pocatello.

Ever trying to move on, I kept sending out tapes and resumes. I received strong encouragement about a chance to broadcast Texas League baseball in San Antonio from the team's general manager, Marvin Milkes. He would later reach the major leagues as GM of Seattle. Milkes expressed a strong liking for my play-by-play tape. But that all fell through when Pearl Beer chose to employ former big league catching star Gus Mancuso, a native Texan and former partner of Harry Caray on Cardinals' broadcasts. Yes, the same Gus Mancuso, my good friend from Houston.

When one is buried in a small market, no matter how extensive his previous experience in a large market, it's difficult to move up. I was fortunate to maintain my drive and energy in Pocatello, working to improve and refine my broadcasting skills. But I never stopped looking to the day when I could again work in a larger market with more pay and saner hours so I could enjoy leisure time with my family. Let's face it, when a broadcaster bounces around in a sea of instability, his family suffers.

Shortly before I was to begin the 1956 season with Pocatello, the team's new manager, Lou Stringer, who had a brief major league career with the Cubs and Red Sox, visited the city. I had met Stringer in Ogden the previous year when he managed Boise, Idaho. Pocatello was operating as an independent team, with no big league affiliation or even a partial working agreement.

I soon received yet another lesson in the swiftly changing fates of the baseball business and how harsh and cold the sport can sometimes be. One night Lou received a phone call from Kansas City Athletics' farm director Hank Peters. Pocatello officials had consummated a working agreement with "K.C.," and the Athletics insisted on naming their own manager. They had chosen former major league first baseman, Joe Lutz. Peters, who would eventually become general manager of three major league ball clubs, then did an honorable thing. Rather than leave Stringer in the lurch, he offered Lou a role as player/coach at the same salary he would have collected as manager.

The 39-year old Lou opened Pocatello's season at second base. Thirty-three year old Lutz was the team's first baseman as the campaign began. It was undoubtedly the oldest pair of players ever to grace a Pioneer League infield. The average age of

CHAPTER 7: ROLLER COASTER...

Pioneer League players was about twenty or twenty-one. Stringer and Lutz truly formed the odd couple!

Lou was understandably way out of playing shape. But the team jumped off to a flying start and after six weeks they were leading the league. Stringer tried his best not to get in Lutz's way, but it was a unique and awkward relationship, with obvious tension. Lutz took it upon himself to change the situation. He resigned, enabling Stringer to reclaim his managerial role.

Kansas City insisted its lower minor league affiliates work out in the morning before they were to play at night. Stringer, ever persuasive and persistent, talked me into pitching batting practice each morning, "I have to preserve my pitchers' arms and Kansas City won't pay for a pitching machine."

Frankly, I hadn't played baseball for 15 years and at age 33 I had doubts about firing (and I use that term loosely) baseballs to strong young ballplayers, but, I couldn't say no to my good friend, Lou. I would pitch about 45 minutes of batting practice, then quickly depart. Players would invariably inquire of Lou, "Is Joe getting tired?" To which Stringer would respond, "He doesn't get tired. He's got to go on the radio as a disc jockey." He wasn't kidding. I did a three or four-hour stint before broadcasting baseball every night…more coffee and Coke.

One day, however, my batting practice duties ended suddenly and permanently. I served up a pitch on the outside half of the plate. The hitter, a sturdily built power hitter named Mike Coppola, shot a bullet right back at me. It hit me on the right thigh. My leg quickly turned color, or should I say colors, including black, blue, red, purple, and, as I recall, a little yellow. I considered myself extremely fortunate, for obvious reasons, and never again did I throw batting practice.

An enthusiastic sponsor once joined me for a re-creation broadcast in Pocatello, not to go on the air, but to watch and listen. An engineer controlled the broadcast from an adjoining room. While a recorded commercial was being played, the red light signaling I was on the air would be off. When the commercial ended, the light would be turned back on and my microphone would again be "live." I normally worked at least a half inning behind the action as the report came over the Western Union teletype machine.

At any rate, Pocatello trailed by three runs going into the top of the ninth inning. They would rally for four runs and take the lead. My guest saw the report of the rally on the teletype machine. Unfortunately, his back was to the engineer's control room and he didn't notice the red light come on. So, just as I was primed to build the ninth inning suspense, as though I was right up with the actual game, the sponsor blurted out, "How in the hell did we get those four runs?" Ah, the charm of recreations!

8 FROM BILLY MARTIN TO TED WILLIAMS

Occasionally, I traveled from Pocatello to Salt Lake City for spring training exhibition games to interview big league players and managers. On one occasion I approached Cleveland Indians' second baseman, Billy Martin, who was immediately belligerent, wondering what I would pay for the privilege of interviewing him. I immediately informed him I wouldn't pay a penny.

"Who's your sponsor?" He snapped.

I answered him cordially, but made it clear I wanted to know immediately whether he would consent…I had no time to waste.

With a sudden change of heart he said, "I didn't say I wouldn't go on."

Since Billy had launched his career with Idaho Falls, I suggested we make reference to that city. He quickly nixed that idea. "To hell with Idaho Falls," he said. "I didn't hit worth a damn there."

Years later I encountered Martin at the Sheraton Hotel Bar, in Rochester, New York. He was scouting for the Minnesota Twins and we had a great time talking baseball. Quick-witted Billy always made for an outstanding interview.

Even though Pocatello was situated in Class C, I broadcast the games of many who climbed the last hard mile to the major leagues. Some achieved stardom.

I recall interviewing a young pitcher named Jim Kaat, who lasted more than two decades in the big leagues and now is an outstanding network broadcaster. He pitched the Minnesota Twins into the 1965 World Series.

A teammate of Kaat in Missoula, Montana was Sandy Valdespino, who also played in the '65 fall classic. I also announced games of an aspiring young Salt Lake City pitcher named Dallas Green, who later became a successful skipper and general manager in the majors.

Pocatello sent infielder Lou Klimchock to the big leagues at age 18. Pocatello pitcher John Wyatt pitched for the Red Sox in the 1967 World Series. Then there was Duke Carmel, who eventually graduated to the Mets and Yankees.

Two Pioneer League skippers, Frank Lucchesi and Jack McKeon, went on to manage in the major leagues. Pocatello infielder Chico Salmon, pitchers John O'Donoghue, Diego Segui, Norm Bass and Dan Pfister all reached the majors.

Another Pioneer League manager I came to know well was Whitey Kurowski, the 1942 World Series hero for the St. Louis Cardinals. One of my all-time favorites was Charlie Metro, a manager for Twin Falls and Idaho Falls, who later piloted Kansas City and the Cubs.

Pocatello's 1957 spring training base was in Huntsville, Texas. I was there a week, during which it rained for six days, although no games were postponed. We were housed in barracks that during World War II had been occupied by German prisoners of war — the veterans of Rommel's Afrika Korps.

It was in Huntsville that I first came to know George "Twinkle Toes" Selkirk, who performed in six World Series, during a nine-year Yankee career under the iron discipline of Joe McCarthy. Selkirk told me the day he first joined New York, he was seated at his locker, putting on his uniform, when Babe Ruth approached him.

At the time, in the gathering dusk of his glorious career, Ruth had become cantankerous and even bitter about the approaching end. Ruth, voice dripping with sarcasm, blurted, "So you're the kid who's taking my place." George responded by saying he would do his best.

Not the least bit amused, the Babe bellowed, "Kid, you'll take my place when I'm damn good and ready to give it to you!"

Ruth was hardly a strong practitioner of the social graces, even in mixed company. Ex-teammate Carl Mays, the pitcher who beaned Ray Chapman, thus causing the only fatality in baseball history, told me some hilarious stories about Ruth. One time the Babe and Mays were in a Boston hotel lobby visiting with Herb Pennock and his wife, the epitome of a refined and gracious lady.

Suddenly Ruth boomed out, "If you folks will excuse me, I've got to take a leak so bad I can taste it." The Bambino walked away without evidencing the slightest hint of embarrassment.

Selkirk had more than his share of unique baseball experiences. In his 1936 World Series debut, he walloped that classic's first home run, connecting off the indomitable Carl Hubbell, who easily beat the Yankees that day. Not only did Selkirk play with Ruth, he also was a teammate of Joe DiMaggio and Lou Gehrig and managed Mickey Mantle when the 19-year-old rookie was sent down by the Yankees to Triple A affiliate, Kansas City. Mantle was so depressed when Stengel banished him to the minors that he got off to a horrendous start and seriously considered abandoning baseball. Once he was so desperate for a hit he resorted to drag bunting and beat it out. Returning to the dugout, Mickey found an irritated Selkirk awaiting him. The manager sternly reminded Mickey he was there to work on his hitting, not bunting. Mantle's response was to go on a hitting spree that vaulted him back to the Bronx, where he reclaimed his right field job alongside DiMaggio and performed in the 1951 World Series.

Selkirk and I hit it off from the first. I spent many hours with him during that 1957 spring training in Texas and whenever his scouting assignment took him to Pocatello, he'd join me in the broadcast booth, an excellent vantage point from which to watch Kansas City's young hopefuls perform. Years later, when I needed a few letters of recommendation to secure a play-by-play job in Rochester, N.Y., I enlisted Selkirk's assistance and he came through promptly. He was a man who handled his fame gracefully.

Baseball scout Babe Dahlgren, who succeeded seriously ill Lou Gehrig at first base when the Iron Man's long streak of consecutive games sadly ended, was a frequent Pocatello visitor. Dahlgren vividly recalled the day in 1939 when he replaced Gehrig in Detroit.

CHAPTER 8: FROM BILLY MARTIN... 69

Manager Joe McCarthy tersely commanded him, "Grab your glove kid, you're in there." Just like that, after the "Iron Horse" had played in every Yankee game since 1925 when he replaced Wally Pipp, who had asked out of the lineup because of a headache!

Others with whom I formed wonderful friendships while in Pocatello were Dolph Camilli, erstwhile Brooklyn Dodgers' hero, as well as Pat Mullin, Mike McCormick, Al Zarilla and Earl Johnson, a man who pitched three times for Boston's Red Sox against St. Louis in the 1946 World Series.

Following one game, I noticed baseball's "Clown Prince" Max Patkin on a dance floor at a local hotel. He tapped an attractive woman on the shoulder and proclaimed in a none-too- quiet voice, "Lady, I don't make a habit of dancing with ugly women, but for you I'll make an exception." The woman, revealing her sense of humor, laughed good-naturedly and obviously enjoyed dancing with her graceful, loose-jointed partner.

Another time the ball club staged a promotion dubbed "Fishing Car Night." The team collected about a dozen ancient jalopies and awarded them as prizes to "lucky" fans. As part of the routine, the cars would be driven around the bases. One of the crippled clunkers, which obviously should have been relegated to a junkyard, made loud and alarming noises on its tour of the basepaths. Just before it reached second base, the old vehicle sputtered and croaked. It all seemed so funny I couldn't contain myself while describing the car's dying journey before it was mercifully hauled off to the junkyard.

Pocatello outfielder, Don DeGroot, was mired in a long and painful batting slump. After feebly grounding out, he raced past first base, continued down the right field line, and in a final flourish of frustration, hurdled over the low outfield fence, putting an exclamation point on the day, and, his brief career.

We even had a marriage ceremony at home plate. And following the pre-game ceremony, the bride expressed an interest in departing quickly, but the groom insisted on remaining for at least a few innings. I knew how the game ended, but never did find out whether that union prospered.

Most Pioneer League players were in their first or second year of pro ball. Understandably, some could be overwhelmed by self-imposed pressure. I saw a Pocatello shortstop, Leo Kernica, become so unglued he committed four errors in one inning!

A fine prospect from Louisiana, pitcher Jimmy Gore, once walked six consecutive batters and somehow remained in the game. I asked manager Vince Plumbo why he subjected Jimmy to such a humiliating experience. Plumbo replied frankly that he had orders from Kansas City not to remove Gore from the game. His confidence shattered, Jimmy was soon out of baseball.

I would develop a strong bond with another Pocatello skipper, Tom Giordano, who eventually became the Cleveland Indians' assistant general manager. Giordano once beat out a young slugger, named Henry Aaron , for the South Atlantic (Sally) League homerun crown. When Giordano joined the Philadelphia Athletics, Manager Jimmy Dykes sent him up to pinch-hit in his major league debut. Giordano looked at strike three. When he returned to the dugout, Dykes admonished him.

CHAPTER 8: FROM BILLY MARTIN...

"Kid, I sent you up to hit, not to look."

Giordano absorbed the lesson well. In his next at bat, he clubbed a home run. Giordano would delight in sitting in on my morning disc jockey program. He liked it so much that I once turned the entire program over to him. He delivered a masterful performance.

Our studios in Pocatello could hardly be described as luxurious and roomy, but they were better than one description: "The outhouse with the antenna."

Pocatello had an outstanding team in 1958, sparked by second baseman Lou Klimchock, who went on to a major league career that included stints with Kansas City, Cleveland, and Washington. Before that season began, the Athletics' farm director Hank Peters told me Klimchock would give the team steady defense at second base and he would hit "reasonably well."

All Klimchock did, despite a painful knee injury that sidelined him for three weeks, was hit .389 with 28 home runs and 112 RBI in only 110 games. Lou was so impressive that in the month of August, long before rosters were expanded in September, he was called up to the big leagues. I doubt whether that had ever happened before...a player during the season vaulting all the way from Class C to the majors. Klimchock was astounded to get the call from Kansas City. I drove him to the airport. Lou hardly had time to pack his stuff. Only 18 years old, he made the flight wearing a T-shirt and blue jeans when expensive suits were the accepted major league attire of the day.

Once, despite rarely having mounted a horse or even a pony, I was persuaded to ride a mule in Pocatello's annual

Pioneer Days parade. I stayed on the balky animal for more than an hour. When the mule during a brief stop planted a swift and painful kick on a Pocatello High School band member's backside, I decided that was enough and enlisted the services of a "designated rider."

Another time, Idaho Bank and Trust, one of my baseball broadcast sponsors, celebrated its 25th anniversary, with an impressive event. Downtown streets were blocked off and an elevated platform was constructed for the festivities. Movie actress Terry Moore, once wed to West Point football immortal Glen Davis, graced us with her presence. I was selected to escort Terry up the platform steps to the improvised stage. I thought to myself, "She's never had a more handsome escort, well, at least in Pocatello."

In 1959, Ottie gave birth to our third child, Mike, a truly blessed event.

My business wasn't confined to the airwaves anymore. I tackled one extremely distasteful task, in utter desperation, when KWIK was floundering financially. Two owners who purchased the station were complete "babes in the woods". They had been successful salesmen of carpentry equipment in their hometown of Belleville, Illinois. But when it came to radio, Bill Woods and Harlan Miles were in over their heads from the beginning. Neither could fill in on the air, even in an emergency, so their contributions were restricted to the area of sales. Both were complete flops as salesmen, yet they chose to draw handsome salaries that rightfully belonged to productive employees. They were a constant financial drain, so banks would often be unable to cash employees' paychecks.

CHAPTER 8: FROM BILLY MARTIN...

I set up a meeting with Woods and Miles and asked sales manager, Bill Adelstein to join us. I had hoped he would lend support to an admittedly drastic proposal I was prepared to make. Unhesitatingly, I asked the co-owners to tell us what their contributions were in sales. "Very little," they informed us. I further told them that for the station to avoid financial disaster, they ought to remove themselves from the payroll in fairness to employees who had dedicated themselves to making the station a success.

Woods was taken aback. It was obvious he didn't like a mere employee suggesting that he, an owner, relinquish his salary. Miles, however, quickly grasped my point and immediately took himself off the payroll. Woods was a hopeless case and stayed on, contributing virtually nothing. I had hoped fervently for additional support from Adelstein at the meeting but he clammed up and let me do all the talking.

Fortunately, we were all rescued, when a St. Louis investor, Marshall True, purchased KWIK from Woods and Miles. True was a prototype bottom liner. You couldn't take him to task for that. While he didn't take up residence in Idaho, he nevertheless made a trip to Pocatello and subjected me to a grueling three days that could best be described as an inquisition. I was forced to give him a detailed account of all expenses incurred while broadcasting various sporting events. These included sometimes staggering telephone company line charges, my travelling expenses such as airplane and train tickets, hotel and meal expenses, rights fees, my salary, and my commission for sales. Suffice to say, the total expenses were substantial. I then had to show True that we had accumulated sufficient sports sponsor income to more than offset the expenses.

Had I been unable to furnish proof positive that carrying live sports events was profitable, I might have been fired. But I was able to prove to True that a heavy schedule of sports broadcasting could indeed continue to make money. Marshall, demanding as he could be, completely respected me as a professional in all areas, so we co-existed without difficulty during the remainder of my stay in Idaho.

One more story involving Harlan Miles: wanting and needing to make some additional money, I approached him about the prospect of making a hurried trip to Arizona in late March to interview major league ball players and managers as they went through closing stages of spring training. If we concentrated on Phoenix and suburban Scottsdale, we could do dozens of interviews in less than two days. Harlan approved of the idea, so I pitched the entire package to a Pocatello Ford dealer named Ed Flandro, who enthusiastically bought it. The station would earn a substantial profit and I would earn five dollars per interview with no limit on the number of interviews I could do.

So, early one afternoon in late March, 1960, Miles and I began a non-stop drive to Scottsdale, about 700 miles south of Pocatello. Our only stop was in Las Vegas for food. It was about 8 a.m. when we checked into a Scottsdale motel, not to sleep or rest, but merely to drop off our luggage.

We headed immediately for the Red Sox' stamping grounds. I toted a cumbersome Wollensak tape recorder and had to find a power outlet to do the interviews from one location. I needed Harlan Miles to help me line up inter-

CHAPTER 8: FROM BILLY MARTIN...

views and bring the players to the exact spot where I had set up. To get the ball rolling, I approached some of the players myself and brought them to my interview site.

I've never allowed myself to be intimidated by famous guests and Ted Williams was no exception. I introduced myself to "Teddy Ballgame", told him where I was from and that I wanted to interview him. He shouted rudely and profanely that he wasn't about to consent to be interviewed. Harlan Miles at that point became enraged. Stupefied, he responded to Williams' totally unprovoked outburst with utter disbelief. He had idolized Williams and was so distraught... he disappeared. This left me with the time-consuming task of roaming all over the field and into both dugouts to persuade ball players to come to my interview location. I was disappointed over Harlan's departure, especially since his role was to help me, so I could do the maximum number of tapes in a limited amount of time.

I interviewed Willie Mays, Orlando Cepeda, Willie McCovey, Bill Rigney, Bill Jurges, Jack Sanford, Jim Davenport, Frank Malzone and Eddie Bressoud, to name a few. Meanwhile, Red Sox officials who had listened to Williams' loud, foul mouthed and boorish response to my simple request, tried to apologize to me for the "Splendid Splinter's" extreme rudeness.

They insisted, "You've got to understand Teddy." I refused, I had no time to try to understand this man-child, I had work to do. The more interviews I did the more money the station and I would make. I truly didn't need to interview the great star...it was only five dollars more after all.

Suddenly the impulsive Williams did an about face and consented to do an interview. He virtually came through the microphone with his enthusiasm. Listening in, a television sportscaster from Providence, Rhode Island, a Red Sox hotbed, asked me, "How did you get that s.o.b. to talk to you? He hasn't spoken to us for days."

Years later I had two other occasions to interview Williams and found him downright affable. We visited in Pompano Beach when he managed the Washington Senators and another time in Winter Haven while he was working with young Red Sox farm hands as a hitting instructor. I still have a tape recording of that interview. Ted had a resonant voice and strong delivery. He would have made an outstanding baseball analyst.

9 A SAD TIME IN THE LIFE OF A GREAT COACH

During our day-and-a-half stay in Scottsdale and Phoenix, I interviewed 31 members of the Giants, Red Sox and Indians, making separate programs of each interview. So in a brief, hectic time, I was able to realize a decent payday.

Curiously, only one player refused my request. He was San Francisco pitcher, Johnny Antonelli, the 1954 World Series pitching hero when the Giants were still in New York. He politely informed me he had become an "isolationist" and would not be talking to any media members that entire year. He was the Steve Carlton of his time. Antonelli had spouted off the previous year about how he hated to pitch in Seals' Stadium, the temporary home of the Giants when they relocated to San Francisco, and before they moved into windy Candlestick Park. Bay area writers blistered Antonelli whenever he complained about the jet stream that sometimes blew routine fly balls over distant outfield fences.

Less than two years later I would move to Rochester, New York, Antonelli's home since boyhood. I met Johnny again right after he retired from baseball. I never reminded him of our Scottsdale meeting. He became a good friend and was a participating sponsor on my broadcasts. He owned at least four Firestone Tire stores, each a thriving success.

College basketball was a dominant part of Pocatello's sports life while I was there. As halftime ended in an Idaho State/Montana State basketball game in Bozeman, ISC coach, Steve Belko vociferously argued with a referee and bluntly suggested where the official could put his whistle. When the teams reappeared to begin the second half, the beleaguered referee misplaced his whistle and a long delay ensued. While the official conducted a lengthy search for the vital piece of equipment, Idaho State player, Les Roh suggested to his harried coach that maybe the referee had taken his suggestion literally.

Belko was a superstitious character who at times carried his idiosyncrasies to an extreme. One afternoon before a game matching his Bengals against Colorado State, I attended a movie with Belko. There came a point in the film, The Rains of Ranchipur when a Bengal tiger was shot. Belko rose from his seat and in a loud voice urged the wounded animal to get up. The poor beast was mortally wounded, however.

Idaho State's basketball team competed in the Rocky Mountain Conference and won the title in all seven of my years broadcasting their games. The Bengals faced many formidable national powers outside the conference. They took on Seattle in a year when Elgin Baylor catapulted the Chieftains into the national championship game against Adolph Rupp's Kentucky Wildcats. Idaho State upset Seattle that season in Pocatello and almost repeated the shocker in Seattle.

They battled the University of San Francisco, which took third place nationally in 1957. The Dons had won the grand prize the previous two seasons when Bill Russell and K.C. Jones reigned supreme.

From 1957 through 1959 Idaho State made three consecutive trips to the Far West Regional in the national round of 16. Each of those years they had to overcome quality opponents in the struggle for an at-large berth.

Principal architect of the Bengals' impressive success at that level was Coach John Grayson; himself an incredible story. Grayson came to Pocatello in the fall of 1956, succeeding Steve Belko, who had taken command of the Oregon Ducks.

Grayson was determined to prove his superior coaching ability. He had done well as Oklahoma University's freshman coach and was distraught when passed over for the head-coaching job by OU athletic director Bud Wilkinson, the legendary football genius. Grayson was on a mission to prove Bud made the wrong choice in Soonerland.

John's 1959 team produced the most exciting finish I've ever broadcast in a basketball game. It took place in Las Cruces, New Mexico and pitted Idaho State against Border Conference champions, New Mexico State. A coin flip determined the site, the Aggies' home floor, where they hadn't tasted defeat in two seasons. Idaho State, decimated by the loss of three mainstays who had fallen by the wayside academically, predictably trailed by 11 points with 3:09 remaining on the game clock. Then came a huge break. New Mexico State's Presley Askew missed a driving lay-up that, had he made it, would surely have spelled the Bengals' demise. Swiftly,

Idaho State mounted a counter-attack led by a freckle-faced, red-headed firebrand named Jim Rodgers, who would scorch the nets for 35 points on that unforgettable night on the New Mexico desert.

Rodgers was a born floor general. Not only did he direct the attack from his point guard post, Jim was his team's foremost perimeter shooter. A crucial moment transpired no more than 20 feet from my courtside vantage point. With teammate Jerry Griffin screening, Rodgers launched a high arcing jump shot that cleanly swished the strings. Just as he fired, a collision occurred, accompanied by the shrill sound of a whistle and the referee's frantic signal that Rodgers' basket was disallowed.

I recall blurting into my microphone, "Who committed the foul?"

Was it Griffin for setting an illegal (moving) screen, or was it the Aggies' defender for pushing off?

"You're pushing," shouted the referee pointing to the New Mexico State defender.

Griffin, who wore glasses with thick lenses, strode to the free throw line with Idaho State trailing by a point. Shooting one and one, Griffin launched a brick that bounced around the rim about three times but somehow dropped through.

Jerry's second free throw was straight and true. Idaho State had its first lead of the contest.

Twenty seconds remained as New Mexico State moved up. A shot went up, hit the front rim and Idaho State's Ray Griffith grabbed the defensive rebound, only to fumble it out of bounds. The Bengals clung to their one-point advantage as New Mexico State set up with 12 heart-stopping seconds remaining.

The crowd exploded in an ear-splitting din as the Aggies worked the ball to sharpshooting Billy Joe Price, who let fly from the top of the key just before time expired. Price's shot barely missed, earning ISC another trip to the regionals in San Francisco.

Before a huge throng, Idaho State gave St. Mary's and NBA-bound, Tom Meschery a great battle before succumbing. The following night Idaho State upset a strong Utah team to gain third place in the tournament. The Bengals had never before achieved that level of basketball success.

Only weeks later, Grayson landed a prize plum, the University of Washington head coaching assignment. Understandably, John felt vindicated after his perceived snub by the Sooners and Wilkinson. Grayson immediately achieved success at Washington, competing against powers like UCLA, USC, California, and Stanford. After years of prosperity, however, Grayson was again battered by cruel misfortune.

Al Lightner, a basketball official who doubled as a sports writer (what a combination) wrote a scathing Saturday Evening Post article about coaches who were poor sports and persistent referee baiters. Lightner included Grayson in his accusations. John thought the article was grossly unfair, but that opinion wasn't shared by Huskies' Athletic Director Jim Owens, who fired Grayson after the damaging story appeared. John was suffering from the early stages of Parkinson's Disease but still could function ably as a coach. Owens, however, used the illness as a reason for dismissing Grayson.

Owens, a former Sooner football coach like Wilkinson, knew John while at Oklahoma.

Grayson retreated into a shell and for several years couldn't bear to watch a Huskies' game. I encountered Idaho State football coach, Babe Caccia at a coaches' convention in New York City. He asked me whether I had heard about John Grayson. His once dynamic personality had vanished.

Grayson never returned to basketball as his health deteriorated. His wife, Maxine wrote me a letter, informing me John had tried to write me, but his fingers wouldn't function on the typewriter keys. Supported by ex-players, including Jim Rodgers, Grayson sued the Saturday Evening Post because of Lightner's defamatory story and collected a tidy sum. But his health grew progressively worse and he died at all-too-early an age. John was a religious man, given to reading the Bible daily. However, he had perhaps without fully realizing it, made a veritable religion of basketball and the sport ultimately devoured him.

I believe that if Idaho State had not rallied to beat New Mexico State, and then defeated Utah in the regionals, Grayson would never have been considered for the Washington job. He might have had many more happy and productive years at Idaho State. I still hear from Grayson's widow, Maxine, now living in Renton, Washington.

Rodgers and many teammates were unswervingly loyal to the intense Grayson. I always enjoyed interviewing the fascinating man on a pre-game coaches' show, although I found him to be cantankerous at times. Grayson was a severe taskmaster, drilling his charges relentlessly.

I once asked Captain Rodgers, "How's John these days?"

"Unbearable," he said emphatically.

Rodgers went on to coach Byron Beck, an all-time Denver Nuggets favorite at Columbia Basin Junior College in Washington. In 1963-64, that team went 27-0 en route to a two-season, 38 game winning streak. Rodgers was inducted into the Washington coaches' Hall of Fame.

College athletes sometimes have a cruel and dangerous sense of humor. On a journey to Bozeman, Montana, the Idaho State basketball team stopped for lunch in West Yellowstone. Most players had already boarded the team bus when Sam Beckham strolled leisurely from the restaurant. Beckham suddenly spotted a huge moose and quickened his pace toward the bus, pursued by the fierce looking animal. The player closest to the bus door let the moose chase Sam around the vehicle before relenting and opening the door to welcome a shaken Beckham.

Another time, sitting down to enjoy a pre-game meal with coach and players, I spotted a worm in my salad, which hardly improved my appetite. Everyone was howling, before I discovered it was a fake. One night, before an NCAA tournament game in the huge, sprawling Cow Palace, Coach Grayson was counting heads during early stages of pre-game warm-up. He became visibly upset when he discovered only 11 players on the court, one too few. Lo and behold, the mystery was solved when happy-go-lucky, but enterprising Roy Cheney, was spotted in the foyer, wearing a topcoat over his Bengal uniform, enthusiastically… SCALPING TICKETS!

One evening prior to a game I asked Goose Crumby, about to play his first college game, how he was feeling. He replied that his feelings puzzled him and he admitted to being rather nervous. As Goose explained it, "One minute I'm constipated and the next minute I have diarrhea." It was the best description I ever heard from a player concerning pregame preparations.

* *

When I announced Idaho State College basketball, the team often played a home and home series with Seattle University. Early in 1961 I met Seattle sportscaster Keith Jackson in Pocatello. Keith told me his station KOMO had secured rights to broadcast Seattle's Pacific Coast League games that baseball season. He said they had already talked to a Spokane announcer, Lee Desilet, about the possibility of their teaming up. Jackson wasn't sure Desilet would accept, but told me the job was Desilet's if he wanted it. Keith suggested however, I give him a play-by-play tape in case KOMO and Desilet didn't consummate an agreement. The next week Idaho State played in Seattle and I paid Keith a visit the day before the game. He had tried not to let my hopes run too high, but when one is trying to advance from a 250 watt station in Pocatello to a booming 50,000 watter in Seattle, it's difficult to restrain enthusiasm. So, when Keith informed me Desilet had accepted KOMO's offer, I felt a deep letdown. What made the news even more distressing was Keith's telling me my play-by-play was superior to Desilet's.

My Pocatello station continued comprehensive play-by-play coverage of minor league baseball coupled with college and high school football and basketball games. Addi-

CHAPTER 9: A SAD TIME IN THE LIFE...

tionally, intercollegiate boxing became highly popular in Pocatello. I did blow-by-blow accounts of all home matches. I had previous boxing announcing assignments in Freeport and Peoria and thoroughly enjoyed doing the bouts. Idaho State's boxing program was nationally renowned. While I was there, the school twice hosted the NCAA finals.

Idaho State boxers like Ellsworth "Spider" Webb, a middleweight, and heavyweight Roger Rouse achieved considerable recognition as pros; good enough to gain title bouts in their respective weight divisions. I went to Logan, Utah to watch Webb duel Gene Fullmer for the middleweight title. Spider was no match for Fullmer's powerful punches and punishing inside assault. Schools including Wisconsin, Michigan State, Syracuse, and Oklahoma regularly sent teams to compete in Pocatello. Idaho State coach, Dubby Holt twice led United States Olympic boxing teams to Gold Medal victories in the summer games; once in Melbourne and four years later in Rome. Holt's forte' as a collegian at Idaho was track and field. He remembered racing against the immortal Jesse Owens.

If I were to pick an interview that stands out, it was one I did with Jack Dempsey. He was in Pocatello to referee collegiate boxing bouts. When I called his hotel room, he enthusiastically invited me to join him. We visited for awhile, then I began taping. He reminisced about his historic battles with Gene Tunney, including the famous "long count" heavyweight title battle at Soldier Field before more than 100,000 wild-eyed spectators. Dempsey, after flooring Tunney, neglected to go to a neutral corner so the count could commence. The brief delay enabled the backpedaling Tunney to clear the cobwebs from his brain and survive the round. Undoubtedly, it cost Dempsey the biggest prize in sports, the heavyweight boxing crown. He lost his head in the heat of combat. Gene clearly outboxed the Manassa Mauler the rest of the fight to retain his title. Like Rocky Marciano in a later era, Tunney retired as an undefeated heavyweight champ.

Dempsey talked about being knocked through the ropes by Luis Firpo, the "Wild Bull of the Pampas." Jack landed on a sportswriter's typewriter, then was literally shoved back into the ring barely in time to avoid being counted out. I felt as though I were sitting in on some of the most exciting episodes in boxing annals. I stopped the recorder and suggested maybe Dempsey might have other things to do.

Jack replied, "Nonsense, I've got all afternoon. Get your recorder going again." So I did and the sheer joy of visiting with the magnetic ex-champ continued.

Dempsey suggested I accompany him on a few stops. I informed him I was due back at the radio station and couldn't join him, whereupon he gave me the key to his room and suggested I rest up, order room service, anything. Unfortunately I couldn't take him up on his offer, but Dempsey couldn't have been more accommodating. Before he left, he invited me to be his guest at a banquet that night. I happily accepted.

I'll never forget my time with the Manassa Mauler. It has been said and written that Dempsey was pure animal in the unforgiving prize ring, bent on swift annihilation of his opponent. He couldn't have been kinder to me had I been a family member.

10 FOND MEMORIES OF HARRY, RED, MEL & HORNSBY

The magnetic voice was forever stilled in February 1998, but fond memories linger. How does one analyze or define the magic of Harry Caray? He was animation and excitement personified. No matter what the score, or the quality of play on the field, there was no such thing as a dull broadcast when Harry was at the microphone. He left an indelible imprint on baseball.

That gravelly voice, which some found harsh and grating, might have been the leading source of Caray's undeniable popularity. It was his most distinctive trademark and accentuated the drama he would naturally inject into his broadcasts. Harry never over-hyped the game of baseball. The reflected excitement came from his heart and endeared him to his admiring fans. Arguably, no broadcaster ever had a more dedicated, loyal following. Caray didn't merely entertain his listeners; he mesmerized them.

Harry wasn't nearly as eloquent or lyrical as the Los Angeles Dodgers' Vin Scully, nor as technically precise as Red Barber. Yet, Harry had a lasting love affair with his fans and listeners. They didn't care about his sometimes outrageous mispronunciations of players' names, but newspaper media critics did. I often felt these critics were jealous of Harry's prestige and earning power. Caray would laughingly slough off his competitors, asking, "What are they so concerned about? I've always mispronounced names." Harry treated it as if it were a badge of distinction.

There were no icons who escaped Caray's unbridled wrath when the Cardinals were struggling. Eddie Dyer had a successful run as St. Louis skipper from 1946-50, including a world championship in 1946. Yet Harry's second-guessing of Dyer was so vitriolic that one of Eddie's sons suggested he punch Caray's nose.

Harry believed in making himself comfortable while describing a game. When I broadcast a St. Louis versus Houston spring training exhibition game in 1953, I noticed that Caray disdained use of broadcast booth facilities. Harry apparently had not absorbed his full quota of sunshine while in Florida. So he described the game out in the open, on the rooftop of Buffs' Stadium. He stripped off his shirt and announced the game clad only in shorts, in full view of about 10,000 fans.

Harry always perceived himself as a fan describing a game. So, it was only fitting that Harry would occasionally venture into the Wrigley Field bleachers to announce the game, sitting shirtless, just like many of his fellow fans.

Harry seldom used complete sentences, but his descriptions provided a crystal clear and comprehensive picture. Listeners could close their eyes and still get a clear view of the action. Caray gave such a brilliant picture, that he was more suited to radio than television. Harry had an abundance of

CHAPTER 10: FOND MEMORIES...

what all good announcers strive for – an ability to transport the listener to the field as the action unfolds.

Once Harry asked me to sit in with him during the broadcast of a Cubs-Cardinals exhibition game in Salt Lake City. I informed him that the water in the Great Salt Lake was so salt-laden that even a non-swimmer like him would remain buoyant. Harry openly doubted my sincerity, telling his listeners, "Joe Cullinane is trying to drown me, like a lot of other people. But it won't happen."

Harry had long been accustomed to addressing a sizeable listening audience. Before the growth of televised baseball, Caray had a huge following on the St. Louis Cardinals' radio network of nearly 100 affiliates. It was the largest of any baseball team, covering approximately a dozen states, some of them in the deep South. In more recent years, he gained daily nationwide exposure on the Cubs' superstation.

Harry was justifiably proud of his induction into the broadcast wing of the Baseball Hall-of-Fame in Cooperstown, New York. He was prouder still of what he considered his legacy, starting three generations of Carays announcing major league baseball including son Skip, longtime voice of the Atlanta Braves, and grandson Chip, who in 1997 broadcast Seattle Mariners' baseball. Harry even told me in an interview that he regretted not changing his name to Flip. Before he passed away, Harry was looking forward to telecasting Cubs home games with grandson Chip. Had that come to pass, it would have made television history when the Cubs played the Braves, with Harry and Chip covering the Cubs and Skip doing play by play for the Braves, all working the same telecast at Wrigley Field.

Never did Harry shill for his team or his employers. He had a deep dedication and respect for baseball, but never looked at the sport through rose colored glasses. Caray freely doled out praise when warranted. By the same token, he would be harshly critical when a player wasn't producing, particularly when Harry was convinced the player wasn't giving it his all. Listening fans aren't easy to fool. Harry's credibility soared when fans realized he was always relentless in "telling it like it is."

Harry never backed away from confrontations with ownership. During the years when Harry broadcast White Sox games, he frequently bickered, first with John Allen and later with Jerry Reinsdorf and partner Eddie Einhorn. When rumors persisted that Allen was on the verge of firing Harry for insubordination, fearless Harry commented, "I'm not going to bother packing my bags. I'll be here long after Allen is gone."

Harry spent 11 years calling White Sox games, then startled the world of baseball by moving to Chicago's North Side after Jack Brickhouse retired.

It has been said that Harry Caray never had a bad day. That's somewhat exaggerated, but he was consistently upbeat. He truly celebrated life to its fullest. Sometimes life to Harry seemed like an ongoing party. Never did he shield himself from the fans, realizing they were an integral part of his life in baseball.

Harry had a kinship with his listeners that few other announcers ever approximate. One stranger offered to buy Harry a drink. Caray's response, "Son, the last time I said no to that offer, I didn't understand the question."

CHAPTER 10: FOND MEMORIES...

Ron Santo, former Chicago Cubs' great and currently a Cubbies' broadcaster, learned early in life he was afflicted with diabetes. Ron works diligently on behalf of the Chicago area Juvenile Diabetes Association.

Caray was once an honored guest at a huge assemblage of the Association. Harry, during an impassioned speech, told his audience that in the crowd was a guest who truly acted as an inspiration for fellow "Juvenile Delinquents!" He called for a standing ovation for Ron Santo. He got that, plus a rousing laugh. Truly, Harry at his best.

Harry could be critical of umpires. Umpire, Babe Pinelli, had just called out a Cardinal base runner after a close play at second base. Angry Caray's response: "That reminds me, fans. I can vividly recall an afternoon last March at Al Lang Field in St. Petersburg, Florida, when Babe Pinelli told me he was contemplating retirement, and, after that last, call, I can't for the life of me figure out why those plans didn't materialize."

Another time the Cardinals were playing the Brooklyn Dodgers at Ebbets Field. A Cardinal batter walloped a long drive to left field, which cleared the wall. An ecstatic Harry was set to go into his home run call when suddenly he saw an umpire waving the St. Louis player back to second base, ruling a ground rule double because a fan had reached out and touched the ball before it cleared the barrier.

Spitting fire into the microphone, Harry gave vent to his wrath, exploding, "Of all the lousy sportsmanship, a Cardinal batter being deprived of a legitimate home run. Gus," he said to partner Gus Mancuso, "I wouldn't be a bit surprised to discover that the Brooklyn ball club planted that fan in that precise spot, just to cover that strategic situation." Mancuso tried to placate Harry, who, wouldn't calm down however, saying," I said it and I'll say it again."

Once, when chauffeuring Harry following a game in Houston, I heard him remark, "My gosh, what beautiful women you have here." Tongue firmly in cheek, I allowed that the city did indeed have some very pretty women. Harry responded, "C'mon Joe, you can always look, can't you?"

Once Harry was victimized by a live microphone that should have been killed. During a timeout in a St. Louis University-Marquette University basketball game, Harry gave what in radio parlance is known as the "Cutaway cue." But the engineer in St. Louis was caught asleep at the switch. So instead of listening to the commercial, listeners instead heard Caray spouting off, "I always did say John Bennington was a lousy coach. I wish to hell they'd get rid of him."

How did Harry's inimitable rendition of "Take Me Out to the Ballgame" seventh inning stretch get started? It happened at Comiskey Park in Chicago, while Caray was singing the famous old song to amuse himself and fellow booth occupants. Sox owner Bill Veeck, unbeknownst to Harry, hooked Caray's booth microphone to the public address system and delighted fans joined Harry in an impromptu sing-along. Afterward, Veeck informed Harry, "Your singing voice is so bad that no fan could be intimidated, so everyone felt compelled to join in." In an interview I did with Harry, I voiced the opinion that if ever he was suffering from laryngitis, and couldn't lead the fans in the singing of "Take Me Out to the Ball Game," the Cubs should refund the price of admission. Harry answered, "I think I was born with laryngitis."

Harry never lacked for self-esteem or sheer audacity. While working in St. Louis, doing radio sports shows, he had a yearning to broadcast major league baseball. Harry disdained going through customary channels in pursuit of his dream. He went directly to the owner of the station that owned broadcasting rights to both Cardinals and Browns baseball broadcasts. Harry boldly maintained in a letter that he could do a better and more exciting job of broadcasting baseball than France Laux, a long-standing institution in the Mound City. Rather than brushing off Harry, the station owner gave him a personal interview and Harry was given the coveted assignment of broadcasting major league games in 1945.

Through the years, I had the pleasure of interviewing Caray several times. The last occurred in Denver in 1995, on his only visit to Coors Field. It was apparent that the stroke he endured years earlier had robbed him of some of his sharpness, his quick wit, and even some of his infectious spirit. It was as though a bright light had been partially dimmed. I prefer the memory of an earlier interview I did with vibrant, bombastic and mischievous-eyed Harry Caray, totally unruffled when a ball player friend of Harry's strolled by and stopped to whack Caray on the leg with a baseball bat. It didn't even interrupt the rhythm of our interview. Harry simply acknowledged the intrusion of Gorman Thomas. Such are the memories of Harry Carabina, who grew up in a St. Louis orphanage and ultimately became an American sports phenomenon.

No other broadcaster in history lasted 53 uninterrupted years at the major league level. Caray never worked a day in the minor leagues. Since he was looking forward to broadcasting Chicago Cubs' games again in 1998, one might say, "He died with his boots on."

* *

I first met Red Barber in 1949 when he enjoyed a heyday as the leading voice of the Brooklyn Dodgers. The Dodgers of Robinson, Campanella, Newcombe, Reese, Snider, Branca and Furillo were arguably the greatest National League team ever assembled.

Working in Freeport, Illinois, I would occasionally journey to Chicago to watch the Cubs or White Sox. I would wait outside the visiting team's radio booth and ask the announcer if I could watch him work, hoping I could learn while observing and listening.

Introducing myself to "the Ole Redhead," I named the city where I worked and the call letters of my radio station. He immediately introduced me to his cohort, Connie Desmond, a brilliant talent whose career was substantially shortened by an addiction to John Barleycorn.

Barber exuded a persona of total composure while broadcasting. He didn't seem calm in those last few minutes before air time, however, loudly berating his statistician for not keeping several pencils sharpened to the width of a Gillette Blue Blade, "…with the shahpest edges evah honed."

Years later, Barber told me he was "ovahwhelmed" by the thought of broadcasting his first World Series game in

CHAPTER 10: FOND MEMORIES...

1935. In those last minutes before zero hour, Barber told himself that, no matter how vast his audience, he had only one microphone and he would focus complete attention on one listener. Those thoughts enabled him to regain total composure.

Barber could make his pre-game descriptions more engrossing than some announcers describing a grand slam homer. He'd say, "As we peer skyward from our catbird's seat, we can observe a few tiny puffs of white against a 'hahd' blue. And man, she's hot."

The inimitable Barber, once the game began, was overflowing with unique and colorful word pictures, such as, "Phil Rizzuto scooped up that grounder just like a hog snappin' up cawn bread, heah?" Or, "There's a towering drive hit deep to straightaway center field. Mantle streaking back, Mickey still goin' hahd and he GETS THERE! Mantle plucked that ball out of the blue sky just short of the Babe Ruth monument."

I never met the esteemed Yankees' orator, Mel Allen, but after one phone conversation I felt I knew him better than many a baseball man I had met. I had written Mel, asking for suggestions on getting to a larger market. He wrote back, suggesting I contact him at the Hotel Del Prado on the Yankees' next visit to Chicago. My Freeport duties precluded my going to the Windy City to meet him, but he arranged for Taylor Spink, The Sporting News publisher, to run three weekly advertisements on my behalf, FREE OF CHARGE.

I remember Mel doing a live commercial for White Owl Cigars that became hilarious when he was unable to suppress coughing spasms. Fans who listened to Mel only at World Series time missed his occasionally cornball approach that he used daily on Yankee broadcasts. Once he introduced partner Curt Gowdy saying, "Now it gives me great pleasure to bring to the microphone my compatriot, alert Curt. Howdy, Gowdy."

As sophisticated, provincial and hyper-cynical as New York audiences tended to be, a huge majority responded positively to everything Mel Allen said. New Yorkers have often been accused of being the world's most territorial people. But you'd never know it from their acceptance of baseball broadcasters whose roots were elsewhere. In the late forties and early fifties four southerners were baseball announcing icons in the N.Y. metropolitan area. The quartet included Barber, Allen and the Giants' Russ Hodges and Ernie Harwell.

Leaving Red Barber's "Catbird Seat" that day at Wrigley Field, I wandered over to an adjoining booth where Joe Wilson was on television. He made me feel completely welcome. His partner was taking a break from announcing chores. He was Rogers Hornsby, by reputation one of the most hard-bitten, controversial characters baseball has ever known.

Often described as the greatest right-handed hitter in the sport's annals, the "Rajah" had a penchant for being refrigerator cold and bitingly sarcastic. Many of his teammates formed an intense dislike for him. Yet upon meeting this legend, I found him to be the soul of congeniality. He even offered me a sandwich and beverage as we visited briefly before he returned to his analyst assignment.

When Hornsby managed Cincinnati, a young hitter just called up from Tulsa was so nervous he had difficulty

CHAPTER 10: FOND MEMORIES... 97

making good contact in the batting cage. Hornsby's inspirational message was, "Kid, I can spit further than you can hit."

Once while managing Cincinnati, Hornsby greeted powerful slugger, Ted Kluzewski, on Ted's return to the dugout after popping out with bases loaded.

Hornsby growled, "Slugger, my rear end. You don't have a gut in your body." Rogers was fortunate the muscular "Klu" didn't strangle him.

When Hornsby managed Beaumont to a successful year in the Texas League, appreciative boosters gave him a night and in true Texas style, they presented him with an expensive new automobile.

His total acceptance speech: "Thanks for the car, folks. Now let's get the game the hell under way."

St. Louis Cardinals' owner, Sam Breadon, once entered the Redbirds' clubhouse, whereupon Hornsby asked his boss to leave, adding, "This is MY clubhouse." Hornsby led St. Louis to a World Series victory in 1926, only to be fired by Breadon after the seventh game.

11 AT LONG LAST A CHANCE TO ADVANCE

Late in 1961, after more than six years in Pocatello, two job offers came within a week. The first was from Albuquerque, which had just gotten a Texas League franchise. League president Dick Butler, familiar with my work, recommended me. I accepted. Less than a week later, I received a letter from WROC radio in Rochester. Friend and station general manager, Jim Schoonover, wanted me for the baseball play-by-play job there.

Because Albuquerque was making its debut in the Texas League and there was no assurance the franchise would be a success, I told Schoonover I would be interested. Rochester, after all, was firmly entrenched as one of America's top minor league baseball cities, with a rich tradition and their Triple A classification was a notch higher than the one in New Mexico. I called Albuquerque to explain the situation and they graciously released me from my verbal commitment.

I met Schoonover and team owners in Rochester and was hired by WROC to broadcast the complete schedule of 154 Red Wings' International League games. I stayed in Rochester for several days, meeting with sponsors and various media people.

I could tell how important the Red Wings were to many of them.

After returning to Pocatello, I still had approximately half of Idaho State's basketball schedule to broadcast and that meant plenty of travel. When I was in Seattle Keith Jackson treated me to a magnificent dinner at a Japanese restaurant to celebrate my landing the Rochester assignment. Keith was still broadcasting Seattle University basketball for KOMO. Next I heard of him, years later, he had become the first play-by-play announcer on ABC's Monday Night Football with Don Meredith and Howard Cosell.

I vividly recall my first International League broadcast. Rochester opened in Atlanta at historic old Ponce de Leon Park. The Red Wing lineup included future major leaguers Pete Ward, Bob Saverine, Sam Bowens, and Tom Baker. Rochester's first baseman was Luke Easter, who several years earlier was an awesome home run walloper for the Cleveland Indians, performing with Lou Boudreau, Larry Doby, Al Rosen, and Bob Feller. I couldn't help but reflect that it had been more than seven years since I had broadcast from "Poncy", announcing the 1954 Dixie Series before departing for my ill-fated experience in Omaha and subsequent drop to the Pioneer League.

The Atlanta Crackers, affiliated with the Cardinals and launching their first year in Triple A classification, boasted future World Series performers such as 20-year old Tim McCarver, Mike "Shotgun" Shannon, Jerry Buchek, and Phil Gagliano. Their opening day pitcher was Johnny Kucks, who orchestrated a seventh game shutout to give the Yankees a World Series championship over the Dodgers in 1956. Atlanta's manager was Joe Schultz. Some players referred to him as Joe Schlitz because

CHAPTER 11: AT LONG LAST...

of the amber fluid he would occasionally imbibe. Yes, it was the same Joe Schultz about whom Jim Bouton wrote extensively and hilariously in the best seller, "Ball Four". The same Joe Schultz whom, after a winning effort, would urge his troops to "Pound some Budweiser."

Rochester was managed by Clyde King, the North Carolina "Professor" who pitched for Charley Dressen on the Dodgers' team that lost the pennant when the Giants' Bobby Thomson stroked his historic home off Ralph Branca.

On that first broadcast I did from Atlanta back to Rochester, there was no available booth space directly behind home plate, so I did the broadcast from the third base side, a workable vantage point but hardly ideal. In order to call pitches accurately, along with location, the announcer should be on a direct line with pitcher and batter to "read" the corners and to determine whether the pitch was, for example, a fast ball, curve or slider. From behind third base the announcer can't consistently identify the pitch, or where it crossed the plate with reference to inside and outside corners.

My most vivid memory was of a monsoon-like rain that caused a one and a half-hour delay. Fortunately for me, George Sisler and George Selkirk were in close proximity to my booth and they had an almost endless number of fascinating stories to pass along to my listeners.

The game finally was decided on a tape measure home run by Atlanta shortstop Jerry Buchek. The Red Wings' starting pitcher, Tom Baker, had a penchant for surrendering gopher balls, prompting a merciless observer to refer to him as "Home Run Baker", after the long ball hitting star who preceded the Babe Ruth era. Despite a growing problem with alcohol, Baker appeared in 60 games that 1962 season, both starting and relieving.

When I departed for spring training in 1962 in Daytona Beach, I had orders to do many taped interviews that the station would air, right up to Opening Day. I proceeded to do so and got them into the mail pronto. Then came a distressed and irate call from Schoonover a few days later.

He asked me, "Don't you ever check out your interviews to see what's on your recorder," he asked. "When we play them back, they keep cutting out. They're useless to us."

Since that was my first assignment and I had sent dozens of interviews back to Rochester in that initial mailing, I was quite upset. It was hardly an auspicious beginning. I took subsequent interviews I did on that same recorder to a Daytona Beach radio station and the playbacks went without a hitch, so I put them in the mail as rapidly as possible. There came another call from Schoonover. This time his tone was considerably calmer, almost apologetic, as he explained why the first batch of interviews kept "cutting out."

A WROC engineer discovered the baggage area in the airplane carrying my tapes back to Rochester was located too close to the aircraft's radar, resulting in the sporadic, almost rhythmic erasure of sound. I breathed a huge sigh of relief. In all my years of broadcasting, that freakish technical problem had never recurred.

I enjoyed meeting and interviewing other managers and players that season. Toronto was skippered by a jovial, salty tongued, ever-feisty little man named Charley Dressen. This was the same Dressen who summoned Ralph Branca from the bullpen to face Bobby Thomson in that unforgettable Polo

Grounds duel eleven years earlier. Dressen was a fascinating interview guest but I soon learned to tape interviews with Charley. It was never easy to predict what he would say.

The pennant winning manager, Jacksonville Florida's Ben Geraghty, was so intense and wound up that it didn't surprise me when, during the following season, he suffered a heart attack and died in the dugout. Geraghty managed Hank Aaron in the home run champ's Sally League days.

The Baltimore Orioles came to Rochester in the summer of 1962 to play the International League All Stars. I divided broadcasting duties with Bill Mazer of Buffalo. Darrell Johnson and Dick Williams, veterans playing out the string as Oriole reserves, both homered for Billy Hitchcock's Birds. Later, Johnson and Williams would both manage World Series teams. In fact, Williams accomplished that feat four times. Not only did he lead the Boston Red Sox from last to first in 1967, his rookie season managing in the majors, but he guided Charlie Finley's brawling Oakland A's to two World Series titles. He also took a talent-shy San Diego Padres team to the 1984 National League pennant.

My partner, Mazer, went on to bigger things as a broadcaster in his home of New York City. Mazer was a talented announcer who possessed a steel-trap memory. He had an unusual background prior to his radio career. He attended rabbinical school. Subsequently, on Jewish Holy Days, I would, if my own schedule permitted, pinch-hit for him on University of Buffalo football broadcasts. It was a treat to work with him during the All-Star game.

Two standout ex-players joined our broadcasts. One was Johnny Antonelli, who was so talented that he spent 17 years as a major league pitcher without having to work in the minors. He had been an 18 year old Boston Braves' bonus baby. If a player received a certain signing bonus in those days, the major league team was not permitted to send him down. Several Boston veterans, including Jeff Heath, were bitterly resentful of Antonelli, taking up roster space on a Braves team destined to win the 1948 National League pennant.

The other former player to visit our booth that All Star night was Vic Raschi, arguably the Yankees' top pitcher when New York won a record five consecutive world championships from 1949 through '53. Like Antonelli, Vic was a strong addition to our broadcast with his insightful analysis.

There are ball players who literally crave the spotlight and sorely miss it when their careers end. Not so Raschi. He owned a business named Valley Liquors. His ego didn't require that he lend his name to the endeavor. I would occasionally drop in on Vic to pick up a bottle of wine. Often all alone, he seemed perfectly content, far removed from famous Yankee Stadium, sometimes referred to as baseball's "Holy of Holies." We would visit and calmly talk baseball. Once he explained how, while pitching, he would use a box, in and out, up and down. Raschi could propel a baseball with intimidating velocity, but due partly to surprisingly short fingers for a man with such a large frame, he never mastered the curve ball. He developed a very workable slider to complement his sinking fast ball.

Clyde King's Red Wings made the four-team playoffs in 1962. Interest in Rochester was so high I did live broadcasts of playoff games in Jacksonville, an expensive proposition. Telephone line charges were about $325 per game, a tidy sum in the

CHAPTER 11: AT LONG LAST...

early sixties. Rochester forced that series to its seven game maximum before bowing to the pennant-winning Suns.

Major and minor league baseball conventions were held jointly in Rochester that December. I spent the entire week taping 83 interviews with the likes of Joe Cronin, Warren Giles, Al Lopez, Ralph Houk, Bing Devine, and Casey Stengel. After I had completed my interview with the garrulous Casey, even though I had much work still to do, I found it difficult to slip out of his hotel room.

I can vividly recall three who refused me. One was Lefty Grove, a mean-spirited but brilliant pitcher who had an astonishing 31-4 record in 1931 for one of Connie Mack's greatest Philadelphia champions. Grove that year compiled a 17-game winning streak. The day it ended he angrily ripped his uniform in a clubhouse temper tantrum. Grove brusquely dismissed me when I approached him.

Another who rebuffed me was New York Mets' general manager, George Weiss. Weiss earlier stamped his considerable input on baseball history by continuing to build and maintain the awesome Yankee dynasty first constructed by Ed Barrow and Jake Ruppert. Players found Weiss extremely difficult to cope with at contract time. When I told Weiss of my desire to interview him, he haughtily replied he didn't do that sort of thing. I made no attempt to persuade him. Had Weiss reluctantly consented, he wouldn't have made an interesting guest, anyway. In order to make the interview informative and entertaining, my guests need to PARTICIPATE.

A third refusal came from baseball commissioner, Ford Frick, who treated me with utmost condescension. I called Frick in his hotel room and he declined to meet with me, even though the baseball convention lasted a week. The pompous commissioner obviously forgot his roots as a sportswriter who had even "ghosted" some newspaper articles for Babe Ruth.

I did make the acquaintance of two other commissioners. One was William Eckert, a retired Air Force General and the essence of politeness. I also conversed at length with Bowie Kuhn, who would join me later during an All Star Game broadcast from Norfolk, Virginia. During one of Denver's bids to acquire a major league franchise, I gave Bowie a tour of Mile High Stadium.

That first summer in Rochester, I even covered sailboat races on Lake Ontario in addition to my daily baseball work. I had been so oblivious to sailboat racing that I needed to start from scratch and familiarize myself with the sport's most elementary terminology.

I also did interviews for several days at the Women's National Open Golf Tournament at the posh Country Club of Rochester. One of my guests was charming Althea Gibson, who first burst upon the international tennis scene by winning at Wimbledon, victorious in the women's singles finals.

When 1963 rolled around, the Red Wings had a new manager. Clyde King had joined Pittsburgh as pitching coach. George Sisler told me Clyde's successor didn't yet have a big baseball name but had a sharp baseball mind. He was Darrell Johnson, journeyman catcher who had performed for six teams including the Reds, for whom he caught in the 1961 World Series. Darrell was mainly a backup, but collected a number of World Series championship rings and, for a time, roomed with Mickey Mantle.

CHAPTER 11: AT LONG LAST...

Johnson was an outstanding instructor. Some players who benefited from Darrell's tutelage during a three-year stay were Sam Bowens, Dave Johnson, Paul Blair, Curt Blefary, Andy Etchebarren, Eddie Watt and Frank Bertaina. Four Oriole starters in the 1966 World Series, Johnson, Blefary, Blair and Etchebarren all played for Darrell in Rochester. A minor league manager's principal objective is to develop talent for the parent club.

A pitcher who performed two years for the low-key Johnson was traded to Oakland. He was Darold Knowles, who appeared in seven games for a winning Oakland A's World Series team, shattering a classic record. Knowles and Rollie Fingers formed the best bullpen tandem in baseball during their heyday with Charlie Finley's rollicking ball club in the early seventies.

I broadcast a Yankees' exhibition game in Buffalo against the International League All Stars in 1963 when New York was riding high as baseball's world champs. I was assigned by station WROC to do several interviews. That posed a problem, because the Yankees were late arrivals at War Memorial Stadium. I managed to interview nine of them for my Rochester sports program, including the M and M sluggers Mantle and Maris, along with Clete Boyer, Bobby Richardson, Joe Pepitone, Tom Tresh, Jim Bouton, John Blanchard and manager Ralph Houk.

They were all cooperative, although I found Boyer and Pepitone quite arrogant. In contrast, Elston Howard approached me and offered to do an interview. Two weeks later, Pepitone made a promotional appearance in Rochester and I did a television interview with him. He seemed like a changed personality, affable and accommodating as could be. Perhaps the fact that he was being paid a tidy sum for the television interview contributed to the improvement in his attitude.

The Red Wings failed to make the playoffs in 1963, but did advance to post season play in 1964 and went on to win the Governor's Cup, emblematic of playoff supremacy. In 1965, Rochester fell short of a playoff bid on the season's final day. So, while he didn't win a pennant in Rochester, Johnson guided three highly competitive teams. The Orioles were understandably happy with Darrell's leadership. Birds' general manager, Lee MacPhail, assured Johnson he'd be back to pilot Rochester in 1966.

Rochester Red Wings officials didn't want Johnson to return. Some said he wasn't colorful enough to sell tickets, and here I thought that was the player's job.

The Red Wings told MacPhail that if the Orioles were insistent on retaining Johnson they could do it elsewhere. With the Rochester working agreement at stake, the Orioles reluctantly told a stunned Johnson his days in Rochester were finished. I thought Rochester officials were grossly unfair to Johnson. I never looked upon his three-year stewardship as a failure. His teams played intelligent, competitive baseball.

Lou Gorman, who would later become general manager of the Seattle Mariners and Boston Red Sox, remembers giving the bad news to Johnson, who was so distraught he burst into tears. When Gorman tried to place Johnson with Elmira, New York, the Orioles' Double A Eastern League affiliate, Elmira officials initially balked, then grudgingly accepted Darrell. He did an outstanding job, then temporarily stepped aside from managing.

CHAPTER 11: AT LONG LAST...

Despite his catching background, Johnson eventually became the Red Sox pitching coach under Dick Williams. He succeeded Sal Maglie. "The Barber's" personality clashed with the irascible, imperious Williams. Darrell stayed in the Boston organization as manager at Triple A Louisville and developed future big leaguers such as Carlton Fisk, Rick Miller and Dwight Evans, along with reclamation project Luis Tiant.

Boston general manager Dick O'Connell had a high regard for Johnson's big league potential and when an opening developed, Johnson was elevated to the Red Sox managerial post. It was Darrell who led Boston into the 1975 World Series, one of the most exciting Fall Classics ever. The Red Sox and Cincinnati's Big Red Machine battled to the final inning of game seven before Pete Rose, Johnny Bench and company finally prevailed.

As I watched Johnson direct his team from the dugout in that World Series, his face a mask of stoicism, I thought back to the trying times when neither Rochester nor Elmira wanted him. After he left Boston, Johnson managed Seattle and Texas before concentrating fully on scouting.

In the early sixties Rochester had a pitcher who threw with frightening speed. Some observers thought he threw harder than any other pitcher in baseball history. Ted Williams, who once stepped into the batting cage against Steve Dalkowski, never disputed those opinions. Dalkowski once tore part of a batter's ear off with an errant fast ball. I remember an experiment by manager Clyde King in 1962 when he was still trying to harness Dalkowski's awesome stuff. King and George Selkirk wanted Dalkowski, in effect, to ignore the batter and concentrate solely on the catcher's mitt. So they put hitters in both batter's boxes, but Dalkowski still couldn't throw strikes consistently. He was tireless. He could throw up to 180 pitches without sacrificing velocity or movement on the ball. Steve wasn't a big man. He stood 5'9" and weighed 170 pounds.

I once saw Darrell Johnson summon him from the bullpen in Toronto with two out and the tying run at third in the ninth inning. Dalkowski threw one pitch. It bounced ten feet in front of home plate and skipped back to the screen. Catcher Danny Kravitz hurriedly retrieved the ball, whirled and fired to Dalkowski covering the plate. Steve slapped the tag on the sliding runner, ending the game. It was the shortest "save" I ever witnessed.

During the 1964 season, old Red Wings hero Stan Musial returned to Rochester, where he played briefly in 1941 during a meteoric rise to stardom. I was Master of Ceremonies for the occasion and I quoted a well-written paragraph from Sports Illustrated that went like this:

"For baseball fans, September is the saddest month. The sun moves south and the shadows crawl quickly across the infields. But for countless thousands of fans, this is the saddest September of all, for Stan Musial is making his last swing around the National League."

Musial told me my reading touched him. He had very sentimental memories of the 1941 season, when he advanced from Class C Springfield, Missouri, to Rochester, then to St. Louis, jumping right into the thick of a Cardinals/Dodgers pennant battle.

12 CHARACTERS OF THE GAME

When Darrell Johnson managed Rochester, he had some strange characters under his wing. One was Frank Bertaina, a left-handed pitcher who performed for Baltimore, Washington, and St. Louis. I knew Bertaina when he was an 18-year-old rookie, unusual in itself at the Triple A level. Frank was highly intelligent, but still acted in a zany manner much of the time. I always felt it was principally an act to entertain his delighted teammates. He acquired an appropriate nickname of "Toys in the Attic." He enjoyed microphones so much that if I let a couple of weeks elapse without interviewing him, he would inquire whether I was angry with him.

Once Bertaina, en route to a 17-strikeout performance, taunted Toledo batter Frank Fernandez, hollering from the mound, "Hey, Fernandez, if you get a hit off me, we'll stop the game and give you the ball."

When television personality, Bishop Fulton Sheen, visited the Red Wing clubhouse, the team was saddled with injuries. Spotting the renowned orator, Bertaina cheerily asked, "Hey, Bishop, can ya play second base?"

Then there was a chunky hard-hitting outfielder, Manny Jiminez. I once asked Johnson why Jiminez wasn't in the lineup as a road trip began. Darrell replied that Manny never played the first game of any road trip. He always begged off because of a headache.

Following the 1963 season I embarked on a brand new adventure, broadcasting American League hockey games of the Rochester Americans. No sooner had baseball wound up than I headed for Peterboro, Ontario and the Amerks' pre-season camp.

Rochester's parent team, the Toronto Maple Leafs, had won three straight Stanley Cup championships and stayed at the same hotel as the Rochester team occupied. The caliber of play in the National Hockey League was at its pinnacle. There were only six NHL teams then. You can imagine the fierce competition for precious roster spots on those squads.

I needed to tape some interviews for my nightly sports programs in Rochester and enlisted the assistance of Toronto's legendary coach, George "Punch" Imlach. He asked me which players I wanted. I began to recite a litany of names, all mainstays of the Stanley Cup champs, like Frank Mahovlich, Dave Keon, Ron Stewart, Johnny Bower, and captain, George Armstrong. Imlach had a reputation of being blunt and hard-nosed. Yet, here's how he accommodated me.

At ten-minute intervals he sent each player to my room, the most comfortable interviewing session I ever experienced. Near the end of my stay in Peterboro, Imlach invited me to accompany the Maple Leafs on their annual "Western tour" to play exhibition games in Manitoba, Saskatchewan, Alberta, and British Columbia. I didn't have time to accompany hockey's kingpins, but I'll never forget Imlach's magnanimous gesture.

Most of my hockey trips with Rochester were long bus rides. Other teams in the league included Cleveland, Buffalo, Pittsburgh, and Quebec City. Typically, we'd play a home game on Friday night, board the bus at midnight, arriving at about 8 a.m. for a game less than 12 hours later. We'd make the return trip to Rochester following the game, then play a third game in three nights in Rochester. I never heard a single complaint about those long bus rides. From the standpoint of mental toughness, hockey players are model athletes. The only non-Canadians who made all the trips were yours truly and trainer, Jack Curran, who ultimately assumed that role with the Los Angeles Lakers, the "Showtime" team of Pat Riley, Kareem Abdul Jabbar, James Worthy, and Magic Johnson.

I spent a great deal of time with Rochester coach, Joe Crozier, over meals and walking the streets following games to wind down. Crozier confided in me that he wanted to get out of coaching. He had tired of the pressure and would have preferred a sales and marketing job with a hockey team. He must have changed his mind, for he remained a coach for many years, heading NHL teams in Vancouver and Buffalo.

Fifteen players from that Rochester team advanced to the National Hockey League; an astounding number. Some went on to NHL coaching careers, including Don Cherry, Lou Angotti, Gerry Cheevers, and New York Islanders icon, Al Arbour.

Cheevers was a fearless goaltender. In an era when facemasks weren't mandatory, I saw Cheevers struck in the mouth by a puck that seemed to be traveling with the speed of a bullet. Gerry bled so profusely that pools of blood formed in the crease area in the front of the net. He was spitting out teeth or portions of teeth like popcorn. Undaunted, he retreated to the locker room. After multiple stitches, Cheevers skated back onto the ice about 30 minutes later to resume his position in the nets. What a warrior! I saw Cheevers a couple of days after he failed to dodge that swiftly traveling puck. Although his rearranged face and mouth looked grotesque and ugly, he refused to let the injury keep him out of the lineup for long.

I also found hockey fans to be an interesting lot. They acted with reckless abandon, almost like an extension of players in that respect. During a game I announced in Quebec City, I witnessed a fan throwing expensive snowshoes onto the ice. Show shoes were a must in that frigid land. I can't recall whether the fan was in a celebratory mood, or angrily protesting an official's call. Another fan in Quebec City so completely lost control that he threw his CAR KEYS onto the ice. Flushed with embarrassment, the fan had to retrieve his keys in the smirking officials' dressing room.

Unfortunately, due to spring training baseball commitments, I was forced to leave the Americans' hockey team just at the time they launched post-season play. The season finally wound down with Rochester's elimination from the play-offs in mid-May. Because of my leaving the "Amerks" during climatic play-off time, the team chose to hire another announcer, one who could give hockey full-time attention during the following season, regardless of how long it lasted.

CHAPTER 12: CHARACTERS OF THE GAME

I stayed close to hockey in Rochester, however, as the team's public address announcer for many seasons, and even worked a telecast or two for out-of-town games. I also returned to announcing college basketball.

In the Spring of 1966, Earl Weaver succeeded Darrell Johnson as the manager in Rochester. Earl was a better than average second baseman during his minor league playing days. He turned to managing at a fairly young age and proceeded to claw his way up through the Baltimore Orioles farm system as a promising skipper. Earl didn't play a single day in the big leagues, although he went to spring training with the St. Louis Cardinals in 1952. That spring Weaver had the misfortune of playing second base behind Red Schoendienst. Earl was not about to supplant a player who one day would be inducted in the Hall of Fame. Weaver succinctly described his hitting shortcomings saying, "The slider ate my bat."

Early in 1967 I latched onto an assignment that was pure joy for a number of reasons including a strong and huge fan following and exciting road trips. I was chosen to do play-by-play for all Syracuse Orangemen football games, home and away. Syracuse was coached by Ben Schwartzwalder. Some of his prize running backs included Jimmy Brown, Heisman trophy winner, Ernie Davis, of Syracuse's 1959 National Championship team, Jim Nance, and Floyd Little. My first year with Syracuse, their number one ball carrier was All-American fullback, Larry Csonka.

Schwartzwalder was a paratroop officer during World War II, jumping and landing "midst the chaos" of St. Mere Eglise, Normandy in the wee hours of June 6, 1944, not long before the Allies' first assault waves stormed Omaha Beach. The college football wars must have seemed tame indeed, when compared to the memories of D-Day. He died in 1992.

Syracuse had an outstanding team that first year I announced their games. Little had graduated, but Csonka was back to claim All-American honors as a rampaging bull of a fullback who dealt bruising punishment to enemy tacklers.

Syracuse went 8-2 in 1967, losing only to Navy and Penn State, where Joe Paterno was in his second year as coach. What a stirring duel that was, Orangemen versus Nittany Lions, waged in Syracuse's ancient, crumbling, but still charming Archbold Stadium, filled to capacity. Penn State's rugged offensive line included one of the nation's premier tight ends, Ted Kwalick. The Nittany Lions' explosive running backs were Lydell Mitchell and Franco Harris. Mitchell later gained fame with the Baltimore Colts. Harris scaled the heights with the Pittsburgh Steelers during the era when they won four Super Bowl championships as one of the greatest National Football League teams of all time.

Syracuse lost a heartbreaker when tight end Ed Nowicki dropped a precisely thrown pass from quarterback Rick Cassata on a two-point conversion attempt that would have given the Orangemen a tie. That tie would have meant a certain invitation to the Gator Bowl Classic in Jacksonville, Florida. Penn State prevailed, 22-20. Deep disappointment was obvious as the Orange dragged off the field. Only five bowl games existed in 1967 – Rose, Orange, Sugar, Cotton, and Gator. All were played on New Year's Day. Penn State got the bid on the strength of its heart-stopping victory over the Orangemen. The Gator Bowl was a prestigious bowl game then. Now the vast number of post season games diminishes the importance of all but a select few.

I'll never forget broadcasting the Syracuse-UCLA game from the mammoth Los Angeles Coliseum. At the time the Coliseum had a seating capacity of 105,000. The Syracuse Network administrators neglected to order broadcast telephone lines until mid-week when they discovered that radio booth space was no longer available. I wound up announcing the game from the Coliseum rooftop. I was so far from the field it was essentially an aerial view. It was impossible to pinpoint UCLA uniform numbers of gold on Easter egg blue jerseys, so I was forced to identify players from position as identified on spotting boards. UCLA had had its national championship hopes shattered the previous week when O.J. Simpson dashed 64 yards to a touchdown in the final minute to give the Southern California Trojans a 21-20 triumph. Ironically, a missed extra point by the nation's top kicker, both punter and place-kicker, Zenon Andrusyshun, came back to haunt the Bruins.

Gary Beban, destined to win the Heisman Trophy that year, quarterbacked UCLA in their battle with Syracuse, and the Orange scored a major upset over the Bruins. Larry Csonka, not normally a boisterous sort and certainly not given to excessive imbibing, got caught up in the party atmosphere at the Hotel Miramar in Santa Monica following the game and downed more than his share of strong spirits. He was to have appeared with the college All-American team, I believe it was on The Ed Sullivan Show, but he missed his flight to New York, and was conspicuously absent on the nationally televised program. Csonka was the fullback on the Miami Dolphins team that compiled the only undefeated season in NFL history, including victory in the Super Bowl.

Csonka was the best football player I saw while broadcasting Orange games. He was a punishment-dealing, battering ram of a ball carrier. It often took as many as four tacklers to halt his momentum. He was also a surprisingly dexterous pass receiver emerging from the backfield.

Syracuse once played Pepper Rodgers' Kansas Jayhawks in Lawrence. Syracuse players became afflicted with severe cramps during the game, including tackle, Joe Ehrmann, who later became an outstanding NFL defensive stalwart. Joe was in such agonizing pain long after the game that he had to be helped onto the airplane for the journey home. In the aftermath, never again did Syracuse's pre-game repast include steak. To this day, I wonder how team physicians could have been so certain of the link between Ehrmann's cramps and the energy-providing steak.

At Navy-Marine Corps Stadium in Annapolis, famous World War II battle sites are commemorated, including Guadalcanal, Bougainville, Tarawa, Kwajalein, Iwo Jima, and New Guinea. My broadcast partner, Red Parton, was obviously impressed as he quipped, "They sure play a tough schedule."

I broadcast Syracuse football for four seasons before our network was outbid for broadcasting rights. The new owner of those rights hired his brother-in-law to do the play-by-play. Nepotism can be a difficult opponent. I was out.

Once during Earl's long reign as Baltimore Orioles' manager, he asked Birds' outfielder, Pat Kelly, what he had been doing lately off the field. Kelly replied, "Earl, I've been walking with the Lord."

With no irreverence intended, Earl responded, "Pat, I'd rather see you walk with the bases loaded."

Media experts consigned the youthful 1966 Red Wings to the second division in pre-season polls. The Wings were admittedly short on experience for a Triple A team. First baseman, Mike Epstein, came all the way up from Class C ball. Center fielder John Scruggs was a Triple A rookie, as was brilliant shortstop, Mark Belanger. Second baseman, Mickey McGuire, and right fielder, Dave May, were tops, and crackerjack catching prospect, Larry Haney, was so impressive with Rochester that Baltimore summoned him in June. The pitching staff resembled a "Kiddie Corps" that included Triple A newcomers, Ed Barnowski, and Dave Leonhard. It was virtually unheard of those days to win at the Triple A level in the face of so much inexperience. The irrepressible Weaver laughed and made jokes about the accuracy of the sports writers' predictions.

Cracking the whip from the outset, Weaver led his youthful charges to a surprise pennant, clinching on the season's final day. Appreciative fans gave Earl and his team an emotional ovation that lasted several minutes. Not to be outdone, the ball club then presented Earl with a bonus check of $5,000 - most unusual and perhaps unprecedented in the minors. After all, major league teams footed the bill for minor league managers' salaries.

One of my most uncomfortable times covering Rochester games occurred when I was broadcasting a game in Toronto. Only a couple of weeks earlier, Hall of Famer, Bobby Doerr, a hunting enthusiast, warned me to be careful should I ever come across a raccoon. He told me those "cute little creatures" could be bad news especially if they happened to be rabid.

A raccoon entered my booth and I lost all concentration on the game. At first the beady-eyed creature contented itself with nibbling on a half-eaten hot dog. Then my microphone cord captured the raccoon's attention, after which he began to move toward me. At that point I vanished from the booth, abandoning both game and my listening audience. I refused to reenter the booth until the raccoon was forcibly removed. A Toronto sportswriter, Neil McCarl, even wrote a story about it.

The next day he asked me, "When you left the booth, did the raccoon take over the play-by-play?" Without waiting for an answer he added, "If so, it had to be an improvement."

Another time, while broadcasting a game, I swallowed a fly and had tears in my eyes while trying to cough it up. I later reflected, "There are some listeners who probably wish I would swallow my microphone. This is a way of accommodating them."

13 BATTLING FOR MY JOB

Weaver was never given to coddling his charges. That included pitchers who were experiencing difficulty zeroing in on the strike zone. Most managers paying a visit to a struggling pitcher would walk slowly to the mound, trying to maintain calm before talking to their hurler in an attempt to settle him down. Not so Earl. More often than not, Earl would bounce from the dugout and stride briskly and purposefully to the mound, energy exuding from every pore. Effervescent Earl's typical messages to his troubled pitchers were models of brevity.

One time in Rochester, Earl rushed to the mound to talk with pitcher, Frank Bertaina. The summit meeting couldn't have lasted more than five seconds. Questioned about it later, "Toys in the Attic" Bertaina revealed what Earl had told him, "Throw strikes or you're gone."

Bertaina, somewhat unnerved and irritated by his bristling skipper, sassed right back, "Alright, I'll throw the damn ball right down the middle."

Earl never really minded a player talking back, as long as the player produced. It was often a sign that Earl had successfully goaded the athlete into a better performance.

In the Rochester clubhouse, Weaver wanted his troops to concentrate on baseball as they readied for the game at hand. You can imagine his visible irritation when he spotted first baseman, Mike Epstein, reading Robert Frost poetry in a corner of the clubhouse. But what could Weaver do when Epstein was en route to a season of hitting .302 with 29 home runs and, most important of all, 102 runs batted in?

Weaver delivered another scintillating managerial performance in 1967. Earl's team was deadlocked with Richmond as the season ended, necessitating a one game pennant playoff. A coin flip determined the site of a one game duel for the coveted crown. Rochester won the coin flip and excited fans flocked to Silver Stadium in huge numbers the next night.

Richmond's pitching choice was a flame-thrower named Jim Britton. Weaver entrusted his pitching assignment to a young fireballer who, only three months before was pitching for the USC Trojans, a hurler so talented he launched his pro career at the Triple A level. This was Mike Adamson's supreme test. For seven innings the rival moundsmen blew the hitters away with pure smoke. The battle was scoreless entering the eighth inning when Richmond broke through for two runs. Bobby Cox, the current Atlanta Braves' manager and his dugout coach, Jim Beauchamp, delivered key hits. With Rochester at bat in the eighth inning, I spotted Luman Harris striding briskly toward the mound. He briefly conferred with Britton, then removed him from the game.

CHAPTER 13: BATTLING FOR MY JOB

Britton still appeared to have good stuff when he stepped off the hill.

Minutes earlier there had been a commotion in the stands below me. I saw medics tending to a man who had to be helped from his seat, then removed from the premises. As for Britton, maybe he had sustained a blistered finger. Or, perhaps, his arm had begun to trouble him, maybe just a twinge in the shoulder or elbow. At any rate, Richmond's bullpen squelched Rochester and the Braves won the stirring pennant showdown, 2-0.

It was only after the game that I discovered why Britton had been removed. The fan who had to be helped from his seat was 50-year old Jim Britton, Sr. He had journeyed from Buffalo to see his son pitch the pennant-deciding game. The elder Britton had been stricken with a heart attack and rushed to a Rochester hospital. Harris had removed Britton so he could join his father in the emergency room. Jim Sr., however, died before his son's arrival.

The careers of Adamson and Britton, principal figures in that great baseball drama, never fulfilled their high promise. Britton reached the majors, but only briefly. Adamson developed persistent arm problems, clung to life in the minors for a few years, then chucked it all to sell real estate in San Diego.

During the 1967 season, Baltimore optioned 21-year old Jim Palmer to Rochester. Jim was plagued by arm problems in the wake of his 15-victory season and World Series shutout over Sandy Koufax and the Los Angeles Dodgers in 1966. Although Palmer was ineffective that partial season and offered minimal help, he didn't permit pitching problems to affect his naturally affable personality. He was pleasant to be around, which wasn't necessarily typical. I've known some ball players sent down from the majors who brought with them the baggage of a dour personality. Some would adopt a haughty "big league" persona, giving the condescending impression that the minor leagues were beneath their dignity.

Earl Weaver, soon to be the Earl of Baltimore, was one of my all-time favorite characters. He needled everyone, including his wife Marianna. One time I joined them at a mini-golf course and Earl drove her to tears of frustration with his incessant criticism.

Once during spring training, several of us were en route to a nightclub where a hypnotist would summon willing participants from the audience to the stage. The club was closed, but Earl informed us we didn't need that mesmerist. He told us he was an accomplished hypnotist in his own right. He looked at me and said, "Come on, Joe. I'm going to put you to sleep."

I immediately dissented but chubby little Earl, ever persistent, persuaded me to be his "patient." So we headed back to his hotel room. I can still hear him whispering as he took me all the way back to boyhood days. Weaver's wife, Marianna, told me Earl had advanced me to the "second stage", whatever that meant. But before whispering Earl could progress further in his determination to put me under, a 92-year old gentleman, Mr. Bill Beeney by name, proceeded to fall asleep, causing others in the room to laugh uproariously. I awakened completely, thus aborting Earl's act. Weaver wasn't happy about being so rudely interrupted.

CHAPTER 13: BATTLING FOR MY JOB

Another vivid memory of that 1967 season; our youngest son Mike, 8, had developed a strong interest in drawing. I had read that Jim Bouton, optioned to Syracuse by the Yankees to work out some pitching problems, was a commercial artist. So before a game in Syracuse I sought out Bouton in the clubhouse to solicit his opinion of my son's drawings.

Despite the fact that he was scheduled to pitch that night, Bouton spent about fifteen minutes studying the drawings, then wrote Mike a beautiful letter, specifically referring to how his people seemed so alive. Bouton advised Mike to develop an interest in many other activities, too. The man who would one day author the best selling "Ball Four" was one of my prime favorites, an absolute delight to interview.

I always prided myself in being able to reflect excitement during my game broadcasts, but be able to calm down soon afterward. Once, long after a game, a friend told me, "You're still excited." When I denied it, he asked, "Then why are you trying to cut your meat with two forks?"

Once, upon returning home from an exciting Rochester game, I was greeted by Ottie, who alarmingly asked, "Where's Susie?"

I had neglected to pick up our daughter following the game. She was still at the ballpark when I arrived home, waiting for her absent-minded father.

A miserably unsettling period occurred after our second year in Rochester. It centered on a switch in radio stations as the ball club's broadcasting outlet. WROC, which first hired me, had carried the games for several years. Rights fees had soared to a point at which management felt it was no longer feasible to carry Red Wings' games.

The ball club turned to Gannett-owned radio station WHEC. Gannett also owned a television channel and both Rochester newspapers. When WHEC acquired broadcasting rights in January, I was caught in the middle. I was very disappointed about terms of the agreement. The ball club and station had to mutually agree on the selection of announcer. I had built up a strong, loyal following during my first two seasons and the Red Wings knew it. They should have told WHEC, "Joe Cullinane will be the announcer, period. If you don't agree with that, we're wasting our time talking."

I felt uneasy from the moment I heard about the arrangement. That WHEC didn't accept me from the beginning could only be perceived as an ominous portent. The Red Wing ball club, good intentions notwithstanding, had placed me in a position of having to play Russian Roulette with my livelihood.

WHEC even demanded I submit an audition tape. What an outrageous affront when I had broadcast well over 300 games the previous two years! But, submit the tape I did. There was no other choice.

A fan, aware of my predicament, solicited hundreds of others who were sold on my work to sign a petition urging WHEC to retain me as Red Wings' announcer. It was a wonderful gesture. Meanwhile, my "spies", a couple of WHEC time salesmen, informed me the station was regularly bringing in candidates to succeed me, one of whom was Harry Caray's son "Skip."

The Rochester franchise enjoyed indisputable prosperity during the time I announced their games. I had no false mod-

CHAPTER 13: BATTLING FOR MY JOB 127

esty. I KNEW my broadcasts had contributed to that prosperity. My cynicism, which had been held somewhat in abeyance, came back with a vengeance. I was reminded vividly of those desperate days in Omaha. Deja vu indeed!

WHEC eventually mailed a press release to my home, containing a story on Rick Weaver, the Red Wings' new announcer. I was in a state of fury, bitterly disappointed that I had been betrayed, but I didn't have the protection of a contract. About ten days elapsed before I received a surprise call from Fred Pestorius, WHEC general manager. He said, "Joe, that release we mailed you about Rick Weaver, have you shown it to anyone?"

My answer: "Only my wife and children."

His response: "Would you mind tearing it up?"

I could hardly contain my curiosity about Rick Weaver. I found out through the grapevine that Weaver had sent WHEC an extravagantly phony telegram. In it, Jack Buck wrote in glowing terms, giving strong recommendation to Weaver as the new Red Wing announcer. Weaver had the audacity to sign Buck's name. The telegram carried strong weight, particularly since Buck had announced Rochester games before graduating to St. Louis as Harry Caray's broadcasting compatriot. I wondered how in the world did WHEC discover that an impostor had sent the telegram?

Here's how. One night at Stan Musial's St. Louis restaurant, Buck and Cardinals' general manager, Bing Devine, happened to meet in the men's room. Devine commented, "I hear you're real high on Rick Weaver as the new play-by-play man in Rochester."

A startled Buck responded, "The hell you say. Who's Rick Weaver? Never heard of him."

Buck's angry juices began to flow. He obviously resented phony use of his name. He called a WHEC official and spat out the story of the spurious telegram. The official replied that Weaver had already been hired and that it was too late to do anything about it. Buck angrily hung up the phone and called someone higher up in management. That produced the desired result. Weaver was promptly dismissed and my job was saved. Had Buck and Devine not crossed paths at Stan the Man's restaurant, I'd have been history in Rochester. Jack Buck had never heard of me, but it was he who years later related the full story to me.

After five very successful seasons of airing Red Wing baseball, WHEC inexplicably pulled out. The ridiculous reason was their consultant's conviction the station should sound the same around the clock. They discarded their best vehicle in the entire broadcasting day in order to play mind-numbing "top forty" records over and over again. What marvelous creativity!

After WHEC pulled out, the ball club negotiated a deal with 50,000-watt WHAM to carry the games. WHAM had previously been the Yankees' Rochester outlet. The boost gave the Red Wings coverage in approximately fifteen states, west to Pennsylvania and Ohio, and from New England to North Carolina. I know people were listening in those faraway locales because one of the sponsors, R.T. French Company, offered prizes to listeners farthest removed from Rochester. The mail response was large and gratifying.

CHAPTER 13: BATTLING FOR MY JOB

WHAM had a bean counter-type mentality, William Rust running the show. He was not a sports fan. His background was in engineering. He served notice that WHAM would not return as the Red Wings' outlet following the 1969 season. This furnished further proof that Rochester radio stations didn't match the fans' enthusiasm and long-standing loyalty toward the Red Wings. Rochester, in all my years there, was consistently one of the prime minor league franchises in organized baseball.

At the time of WHAM's rebuff, FM radio had come into its own and the Red Wings signed a deal with WROC-FM. All but one sponsor, Genesee Brewing Company, agreed to participate. The sales and marketing people had no objections to the switch to FM, figuring the listening audience would make the adjustment. But Genesee's egotistical and shortsighted owner Jack Wehle wouldn't be associated with FM and steadfastly refused to consider participation. It turned out to be a colossal blunder on his part.

We all know how baseball and beer sponsorship are compatible. Utica Club Beer welcomed the opportunity to step in and fill the sponsorship void. Not only did Genesee forfeit the natural kinship between their product and a proven loyal and large listening audience, but they would no longer be permitted to sell their beer in the Rochester ballpark. Genesee sales manager, Bill O'Connor, wanted me to intercede with the ball club the following season in an effort to restore Genesee's participating radio sponsorship but there was no chance of that occurring. Utica Club was all too happy with the arrangement to even consider surrendering a valuable advertising vehicle. And you can imagine how pleased

Utica Club was to sell its product to Rochester fans, not only listeners, but those at the stadium.

The loss of Genesee's sponsorship proved to be a strong jolt to my earning power. For years, especially during fall and winter months, I was a Genesee spokesman. I served both as master of ceremonies and principal speaker at countless service club lunches, dinners, banquets and sports gatherings through much of New York state. I would occasionally appear at the same banquet with two other members of Genesee's stable of speakers. One was Jimmy Crowley, left halfback in the fabled Four Horsemen backfield at Notre Dame under Knute Rockne. The other was Carmen Basilio, who won both welterweight and middleweight world boxing championships. I made a substantial sum of money making these speaking appearances. Unfortunately for me, Utica Club didn't involve itself with forming a speaker's bureau.

Luke Easter, a fabled Cleveland Indians' home run slugger in the late forties and early fifties, closed out his long-playing career in Rochester. He was a laugh-provoking speaker who could regale any audience with his stories. We often teamed up at the small banquets. Luke's charming wife, Virgil, was studying to be a court reporter when Easter played for the Red Wings. She informed me she would derive valuable practice by taking shorthand of my broadcasts.

14 PINCH-HITTING FOR HANK AARON

One night in Auburn, New York, Hank Aaron was the principal speaker and I was the Master of Ceremonies. I was pressed into service for a long-winded speech as Aaron's pinch-hitter, because Hank was about forty-five minutes tardy. I was doing my best to entertain and occupy an increasingly impatient gathering. I'll never forget Aaron's first lines when he made his belated appearance.

"Don't blame me, folks. Blame Mohawk Airlines."

On another occasion, a lady approached me following a banquet and said, "Oh, Mr. Cullinane, I enjoyed your presentation so much, but I must say I was soooo surprised to see you. I had been under the impression you were a young man." So, too, did I until she disabused me of that notion.

Once I journeyed to Glens Falls, New York, a beautiful city at the southern edge of the Adirondack Mountains. The speaker's platform was sufficiently elevated above the head table so that it could create a definite problem if the speaker needed to say something confidential to a head table member. The Master of Ceremonies gave me a glowing introduction that went something like this: "We're all familiar with our speaker.

You've heard him announce Rochester Red Wings' baseball, he has done professional hockey and University of Rochester basketball. Ladies and gentlemen, it gives me great pleasure to present tonight's speaker——"

He repeated himself two or three times and his voice grew increasingly more subdued.

My wife was eating in an adjoining room, but she couldn't see the speaker. A curtain separated the banquet room from the remainder of the restaurant. She thought the poor man might even be suffering a heart attack. It was nothing that serious. The embarrassed Master of Ceremonies couldn't remember my name. Since my chair was well below the speaker's platform, I couldn't render badly needed assistance. Finally, when it became obvious he wouldn't recall my name, I joined him on the platform and introduced myself.

It's important to maintain a confident frame of mind when speaking. It's equally important never to be arrogant or condescending toward your audience. Yet the reality is that you know more about your subject matter than does the audience. That, after all, is why you're facing them. It's imperative that you make constant eye contact with your audience. Don't focus on a particular area. Continue to look at every section of the room.

Most speakers don't acquire composure overnight. I remember delivering a high school speech. In the audience was my instructor, a rugged disciplinarian who understood the importance of maintaining aplomb while speaking. At one point I lost my train of thought. As if by reflex action, my hand went to my head, an absolute no-no.

At this point the instructor fairly shouted, "Ten points off. Continue." Responding to the challenge, I immediately regained my composure. It was a painful but valuable lesson.

CHAPTER 14: PINCH-HITTING FOR HANK AARON

I recall speaking to a sizeable group of firemen at their station in Hilton, New York. Right in the middle of my presentation, the entire assemblage walked out without offering an explanation. I was left standing all alone until one of the last members to depart informed me they were answering a summons to extinguish a neighborhood fire.

By design my speeches never exceed thirty minutes, customarily followed by a question and answer session. Almost always I work without notes. Why? It's important to maintain eye contact with the audience and any deviation from that lessens the impact of the speech. I never even attempt to deliver any profound messages. My role is to entertain. I discovered I could do that just by telling some of the bizarre stories that inevitably happen when one is doing play-by-play or interviews. Very rarely do I tell canned jokes. That has never been my forte.

It's important that a sportscaster, particularly a baseball broadcaster who is with his listeners for as many as seven days a week, speak at least occasionally at sports functions. There's no better way for an announcer to keep his finger on the listener's pulse. You can learn about what fans like to hear during a broadcast and discover areas where you might be coming up short. What listeners in all age groups want most is to be entertained. They don't want a dry, matter-of-fact account of the action. If you describe the action vividly and thoroughly, listeners will absorb the sport's nuances automatically. A broadcaster's style is personal and unique. Just do what comes naturally and let that define your style.

As for interviews, don't ever let them deteriorate into a straight question and answer format. Let the interview evolve into a conversational mode so that the guest and, ultimately, the listeners won't even be thinking strictly in terms of who's asking the questions and who's supplying the answers. The interviewer need not always ask a question. Often just a comment will give the guest reason to respond. Always focus on the guests, ever ready to draw them out, first making certain they're comfortable talking with you. The greatest compliment a guest can give me is to say, "I really enjoy talking with you. You ask interesting questions."

When you're fortunate to elicit such a response, you may reasonably assume your listeners also enjoyed the interview. It's normally not necessary to rehearse with a guest what you'll discuss, regardless of the anticipated length of the interview. Just tell the guest you'll be guided by his answer to the preceding question. Convey that it's simply a matter of two people enjoying a conversation.

At times it's prudent or even necessary to spend a few minutes with your guests before interviewing them. During a Red Wing broadcast, the team asked me to interview a Japanese ambassador. I was assured the ambassador spoke fluent English and was fully conversant with the game of baseball. After all, baseball is nearly as much Japan's national sport as ours. I felt very comfortable about working him into the broadcast, until my first question. I asked him to give me his first impressions of Silver Stadium. His answer floored me.

Smiling, he said, "I think Joe DiMaggio, he very good baseball player."

It's best not to invite guests on the air during a baseball broadcast too frequently. It can detract from play-by-play continuity. There are some notable exceptions, people who enhance any broadcast for a variety of reasons.

CHAPTER 14: PINCH-HITTING FOR HANK AARON

Rocky Marciano, the undefeated heavyweight boxing champion, joined me for about an hour as I re-created a Rochester road game. He revealed his love for baseball and said he once dreamed of playing the sport professionally. A catcher from Brookline, Massachusetts, he was given a serious tryout by the Chicago Cubs. He said baseball was his first love and that he turned to boxing because of the obvious financial opportunities that sport presented.

Another time, Bishop Fulton Sheen, the renowned TV orator, spent several innings with me in the broadcast booth. His love and keen understanding of baseball were quickly revealed. What a humble man he was. He invited two players and me to join him for dinner at his Diocesan home. The players, Fred Valentine and Bernie Smith, eagerly accepted. Then, in a display of childish irresponsibility, they backed out shortly before the dinner. When I arrived alone, Bishop Sheen's assistant greeted me and was miffed that neither ball player had accompanied me. But when I met the Bishop and he, too, noticed I was alone, he responded calmly and graciously, never evidencing a hint of disappointment. What an object lesson it was for his youthful, impatient assistant. I still remember Bishop Sheen's shining, piercing, deep-set eyes.

Already in his seventies, the Bishop appeared to be in splendid physical condition. He talked about playing tennis frequently on the broadcasts. I kiddingly asked, "Doubles?" He feigned being affronted by the question and quickly assured me he played SINGLES.

He recalled the 1924 World Series during which a bad hop eluded New York Giants' third baseman, Freddie Lindstrom, opening the gates for the Washington Senators and Walter Johnson to win the championship.

Bishop Sheen's quarters were modest, almost austere, for a man of his stature. He lived in a small apartment above Rochester's Catholic Youth Organization center. After we had dinner, I stayed for perhaps half an hour. Then, cognizant of what must surely have been a busy schedule, I was in the process of bidding him good evening. He replied, "Please stay longer. We have much to discuss."

And so I did, for a long while. I remember his describing an acute stuttering problem that once afflicted him before he was able to conquer it. As I prepared to depart, he presented me with three of his books, accompanied by an autographed message.

Ex-managers such as Eddie Stanky, Eddie Sawyer, and Danny Murtaugh lent their vast expertise to my broadcasts. All had World Series experience; two as managers, one as a player.

Actor Peter Lawford was a Rochester visitor for an entire day. He was there to promote the John F. Kennedy Library in conjunction with the Red Wings, so I spent a considerable part of the day with the famous British actor. During a rain delay, I interviewed him at length during my broadcast. I remember him telling how indebted he was to Charles Laughton for his teaching and advice.

A gusting wind blew many of my statistical notes and commercial material out of the booth that night. I would have been in a severe predicament had not the material been retrieved. Seeing I couldn't leave my broadcast perch, Lawford ventured into the rain (after all, he was from Great Britain) and onto a rooftop which dangerously sloped downward and rescued every one of my precious notes, a gallant gesture. Lawford was a gracious and most welcome guest.

▲ Joe Cullinane, age 14, Summer of 1937, Chicago Times Jr. Sports Writer Contest.

▲ Joe's and Ottie's wedding, April 14, 1951.

▲ 1953—Interviewing George Wright, Houston Press Sports Editor.

▲ 1968—Joe preparing to broadcast Kodak College Basketball classic.

▲ 1970—Interviewing two legends of college football, Bud Wilkinson of Oklahoma and Duffy Daugherty of Michigan State.

▲ 1970—Cal Ripken Sr. at Silver Stadium, Rochester, NY.

▲ 1972—Interviewing Mickey Mantle in Rochester, NY.

▲ 1995—Interviewing Hall of Fame manager, Earl Weaver

▲ 1995—My induction into the Rochester Red Wings Hall of Fame

▲ 1995—Accepting Hall of Fame plaque from Joe Altobelli, manager of 1983 World Champion, Baltimore Orioles.

▲ 1996—Me with Bobby Grich at Red Wings reunion.

▲ 1998—Interviewing with Mark McGuire at Coors Field.

▲ 2000—Talking with Cards manager, Tony LaRussa at Coors Field.

▲ 2000—Behind the batting cage at Coors Field with Tony Perez of the Big Red Machine.

▲ 2000—Chatting with Atlanta Braves manager, Bobby Cox at Coors Field.

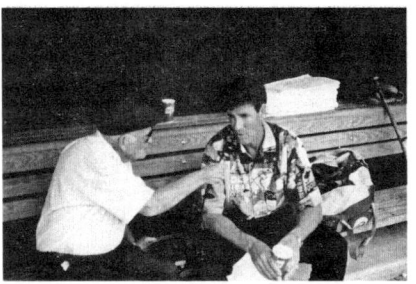

▲ 2000—Interviewing Hall of Fame pitcher, Jim Palmer.

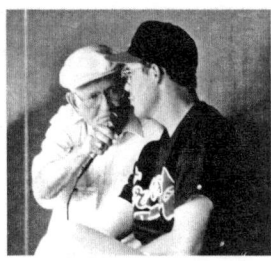

▲ 2000—Interviewing Braves pitcher, Greg Maddux in Atlanta dugout.

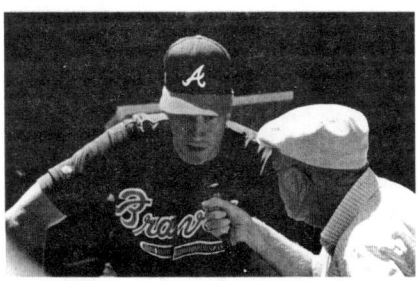

▲ 2000—Tom Glavine at Coors Field.

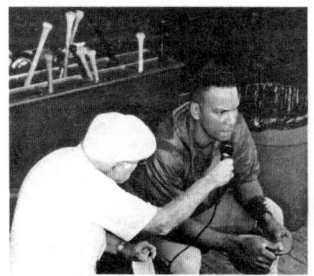

▲ 2000—Interviewing Astros Moises Alou, Coors Field, 2000.

▲ 2001—Talking with immortal Dodger announcer Vin Scully in the booth at Coors Field.

▲ 2002—Posing with Rockies first baseman, Todd Helton.

▲ 2002—Posing with Rockies center fielder, Juan Pierre.

▲ 2002—Hanging around the batting cage with Rockies right fielder, Larry Walker.

▲ 2002—Me and Rockies manager, Clint Hurdle posing behind batting cage at Coors Field.

▲ 2002—Yankees third baseman, Robin Ventura and me at Coors Field.

▲   2002—Talking with Yankees first baseman, Jason Giambi, at Coors Field.

▲   2002—At the cage with Yankees Allstar shortshop, Derek Jeter.

▲   2002—Chatting with National Hockey League and New York Mets announcer, Gary Thorne.

▲   2002—Posing with all-time home run leader, Barry Bonds at Coors Field.

15 MY BIG CHANCE

When Rochester was eliminated from the 1967 playoffs at Columbus, little did I know that would be the last of charismatic Earl Weaver as Red Wings manager. Earl was summoned to Baltimore as the Orioles' first base coach for 1968, hired over the objections of manager, Hank Bauer.

Early that same year, I read a newspaper story that Joe Garagiola was relinquishing his post as a Yankees' announcer to join NBC's Today Show full time. That precipitated a chain reaction. Frank Messer, one of the Orioles' broadcasters, was chosen to replace Garagiola in New York, thereby opening a spot on the Orioles' announcing team that already included Chuck Thompson and Bill O'Donnell. Feeling completely ready for the majors, particularly after broadcasting games of Baltimore's top affiliate for six seasons, I immediately called Orioles' GM, Harry Dalton, a man familiar with my work in Rochester.

Dalton was quick to explain that he would not be involved in the selection of Messer's successor, but urged me to contact Bill Costello, advertising director of National Brewing Company, which not only owned the Orioles but sponsored broadcasts of Birds' games. I wrote Costello, sending a resume and play-by-play tape to him in Baltimore. Shortly afterwards, Costello invited me to come to Baltimore to meet with him. He praised my play-by-play work. You can imagine how excited and optimistic I was when I boarded the plane. Finally, the majors!

Costello told me it was important to know how I would mesh with each of the two veteran announcers, Thompson and O'Donnell. He wanted me to broadcast a spring training game with each of them on the far-flung Orioles' network.

After we adjourned the meeting for lunch with traditional crab cakes, Costello pointedly asked me why I wanted to move to Baltimore. I told him it had long been my ambition to broadcast major league baseball and that I sincerely liked Baltimore. I had visited the city while broadcasting American Hockey League games back to Rochester.

We picked a weekend when I would be free. I knew the Orioles' mainstays; including Jim Palmer, Wally Bunker, Dave McNally, Boog Powell and the Robinsons (Brooks and Frank), from exhibition game trips to Rochester. Others, including Dave Johnson, Curt Blefary, Andy Etchebarren, Eddie Watt, Dave Leonhard, Mark Belanger, and Paul Blair, I knew very well from their Rochester playing days.

Upon my arrival in Miami, I was greeted by manager, Hank Bauer, at the McAlester Hotel team headquarters. He extended a warm welcome, inviting me to join him and his wife, Charlene, for a drink or two at the hotel bar.

Hank had a memorable playing career. He was a New York Yankees mainstay on the only team to win five consecutive world championships. He was a teammate of two of the greatest legends in baseball history, Joe DiMaggio and Mickey Mantle. He played for the immortal Casey Stengel. Bauer still holds the record of hitting in seventeen consecutive World Series games. Twice he managed for the eccentric and egotistical Charlie Finley, once in Kansas City and once in Oakland. Only two seasons earlier, he had managed Baltimore to its first World Series championship.

While I was in Miami preparing for my "chance of a lifetime", Rochester sports columnist, George Beahon, broke the story of my upcoming Orioles' broadcast tryout. The following morning I boarded the Orioles' charter for Tampa, where Baltimore played Cincinnati on the first stop. I spent time with old friend, Earl Weaver. A tenseness existed between Earl and Hank Bauer. Baltimore had experienced a disappointing season in 1967, so one could hardly blame Bauer for casting anxious glances over his shoulder. Hank must have realized that if Baltimore got off to a stumbling start in 1968, his employment might be jeopardized.

St. Petersburg was our second stop as the Orioles went against Gil Hodges' New York Mets. The following day we journeyed to Sarasota, where the Orioles completed their trip against the White Sox. While there I enjoyed a good visit with my old Chicago friend, Bob Elson, long-time Sox voice.

Two nights later it was time for my own personal "D-Day." I had been a sportscaster for 21 years. Now came time to put everything on the line in my bid to reach the major leagues. The Orioles played Ralph Houk's New York Yankees that night and I felt a keen sense of anticipation, even exhilaration, as airtime drew nigh. Down on the dirt and grass, the irrepressible Weaver asked me, "Hey, Joe, what if you start to talk and nothing comes out?" It was an obvious attempt to get me in a relaxed frame of mind.

When I visited the Yankees' dugout, I saw coaches Frank Crosetti, who played with Babe

Ruth, and many of the New York legends, and Jim Turner milling around. I also ran across the famous "Major," Ralph Houk. Mickey Mantle and Joe Pepitone were there, too. The Yankees were wearing their familiar, almost austere black and gray road uniforms with big block letters NEW YORK across the shirt front.

Ascending the stairs, I met two Yankee announcers, affable Phil Rizzuto and the popular "Master of the Malaprop," Jerry Coleman upstairs in the booth. Our engineer gave the customary "countdown" on the Orioles' network as we moved into the last few minutes before airtime. Suddenly, Chuck Thompson was setting the scene, giving starting lineups and other pertinent information. My adrenaline was flowing freely. I was pumped up.

Billy Monbouquette was New York's starting pitcher. White Sox right hander Bruce Howard concluded his warm-ups and Thompson, a familiar World Series and National Football League voice, introduced me.

For a moment, I felt anew that strange, all alone feeling as the Yankees' lead-off batter, Jerry Kenney, stepped in. I quickly settled into play-by-play and time passed rapidly during my 4 1/2 inning stint before I turned the microphone back to Thompson, who is now a member of the baseball broadcasters' Hall of Fame in Cooperstown. I did background

CHAPTER 15: MY BIG CHANCE

color while Thompson rattled off the play-by-play description and felt relaxed working alongside him. Then as the game ended, Thompson turned the microphone back to me for the post game recapitulation. I felt a feeling of satisfaction, secure in the belief I had done well in my first Baltimore network broadcast. I didn't attempt to kid myself, but felt confident the broadcast had gone without a hitch. One more game to go.

The next night, the Orioles hosted Detroit at Miami Stadium. This was an outstanding Tigers' team that included Dennis McLain, who would win the astounding total of 31 games and Mickey Lolich, destined to chalk up three World Series victories, including the climactic finale against Bob Gibson and the St. Louis Cardinals. Detroit's wrecking crew included Al Kaline, Norm Cash, Jim Northrup and Willie Horton. Before the game, for the first time ever, I met Ernie Harwell. The legendary broadcaster made it a point to come to the booth and introduce himself to me. I remember him saying he was familiar with the pressures in broadcasting but never had he known a time when so much was riding on performances in just two games. I felt encouraged after Ernie's visit.

Inevitably airtime arrived again. The seconds ticked down and with a pointed signal from our engineer, I opened the network broadcast with team records, ballpark dimensions, temperature, weather and starting lineups. This was pertinent information I would typically pass on to my listeners during a minor league broadcast. Finally, I talked about starting pitchers, Joe Sparma and Jim Hardin, before calling Bill O'Donnell to the microphone. I handled color the first 4

1/2 innings, then switched to play-by-play during the second half of the game.

After we concluded the broadcast, I came upon Frank "Trader" Lane, renowned as general manager of five big league ball clubs. The nickname stemmed from an astoundingly large number of player trades he negotiated. Frank was bubbling enthusiastically. He had heard my two broadcasts on a transistor radio. A Miami radio station was on the Orioles' far-flung network.

He informed me, "Your friend, Harry Dalton, made sure that both owner, Jerry Hoffberger, and general manager, Frank Cashen, were within earshot of a transistor radio when you were on play-by-play." Furthermore, according to Lane, Dalton overheard Cashen remarking to Hoffberger, "We'd have a helluva time beating this guy on play-by-play."

The following morning I ran across Cashen in the hotel lobby. He invited me to join him for breakfast. He couldn't have been friendlier, further buoying my hopes. I headed for Miami Stadium to say a few goodbyes and was introduced to Hoffberger. Then I made my getaway to Daytona Beach, the Red Wings' spring training home.

It would be several weeks before I would learn my fate. Why? The Orioles wouldn't begin intensive television coverage until early May, and wouldn't require a third "voice" during the season's first month.

Brooks Robinson, my seating companion on one of the Orioles' exhibition game flights, told me before I ever went on the air, "If you think waiting until Friday night tests your patience, just imagine what it will be like after your two broad-

CHAPTER 15: MY BIG CHANCE

casts, waiting weeks 'til you find whether you'll be the lucky man." Brooks was indeed perceptive.

Joining me in Daytona Beach, Frank Lane suggested I write Costello a brief letter, informing him of my itinerary over the next few weeks, just so he could reach me on short notice; I did. I would travel to Richmond, Virginia, then to Buffalo and Syracuse.

Wally Bunker, like Jim Palmer, was plagued by arm problems after pitching a 1966 World Series shutout. Optioned to Rochester, he was the Red Wings' opening night pitcher in 1968. It was so chilly in Richmond that Bunker insisted I wear his heavy jacket while broadcasting the game.

As the weeks passed, just as Brooks Robinson had predicted, I found waiting difficult with the stakes so high. For years I had yearned for a major league opportunity, and the one I wanted more than any other was a spot with the Orioles. It was six weeks before I would find if the burning ambition of my long career would be finally realized—broadcasting in major league baseball. I was just past my 45th birthday, but I knew I had finally arrived at my career crossroads. I had a hunch that this was going to be it. With a certain amount of reserved melodrama, I began to picture myself in this job.

The cards were certainly stacked in my favor. I felt positive that I had done well on both the broadcasts. Nothing beats being there every day, and I was bringing 21 years of play-by-play experience to the table. My thoughts soared as I recalled my meeting in Baltimore with Bill Costello at National Brewing Company. He was enthusiastic about my qualifications and explained why he had wanted me to do the two exhibition games in Miami. He needed to have those as a kind of final screen test, to see how I blended with Chuck Thompson and Bill O'Donnell. We had meshed as though I had been their broadcasting sidekick for years. The job was going to be mine.

For six seasons I had been play-by-play announcer for all home and road games of the Rochester Red Wings; Baltimore's top minor league affiliate. What better apprenticeship? I had all the credentials, but what buoyed my spirits the most during the agonizing waiting period was that owner Jerry Hoffberger was much impressed by my baseball announcing. This was praise not lightly given. Also, I liked the idea that both sponsor and ball club were under the same ownership. That leaves one less group to please.

A willingness to settle for the minor leagues just wasn't part of my makeup. I knew I had major league broadcasting ability and I was pleased that it had finally been recognized at exactly the right time of my life. For me and my family, moving to Baltimore was the answer to our prayers. So, although the weeks of waiting passed slowly, my thoughts had a new and pleasant direction, a settled feeling full of promise. My wife was planning the Baltimore move making the time pass a bit faster for her. For me, continuing with the Rochester broadcasts didn't dampen my desire to broadcast big league games. It was time well spent. I did the work with pride knowing that it would reflect on my future work; that I had not slacked off while leaving the minors to go big time. All those years bouncing around in the lower minors shoveling sand had paid off. I had paid my dues and the contract was only days away.

CHAPTER 15: MY BIG CHANCE

When the big day finally came in May, I had lived a lifetime. I was ready. Already some of my associates and friends had heard the inside track, that I was the new announcer for the Orioles. It was still nerve-wracking to wait for the official word to come down. All your doubts and fears come into play. "Maybe if I don't land the assignment the doors of broadcasting will be closed to me forever," I thought morosely. My friends kept me afloat saying, "Hang on, Joe, you've got it. Who else would they choose?" And then the hour struck.

In early May, the call came from Costello. My heartbeat accelerated from the mere act of picking up the phone. Within seconds, I learned my fate. I remember shaking uncontrollably when Costello told me "they" decided on someone else as the new Baltimore Orioles' broadcaster. Costello further informed me that every baseball man in the Oriole organization had recommended me for the job. He voiced his opinion that my play-by-play was "crisp and clear" and wished me good luck. I was so devastated it was as though my heart had plummeted to my shoestrings. It would be accurate to state I felt despondent, utterly crestfallen.

I soon learned that Jim Karvellas, one of four announcers who participated in on-air "auditions", was Costello's choice, even though Karvellas was a STRANGER to baseball announcing. I felt an enormous letdown. Without mincing words, I told Costello, in naming Karvellas, that he had made an utter mockery of my many years of doing baseball play-by-play.

Years later, the full story was related to me by Joe Bride, who had been the Orioles' public relations director in 1968. In that role he was privy to the entire bizarre story. After

Frank Messer had left for the Yankees, Costello declared at a meeting he had "just the right man" to replace Messer, Jim Karvellas. The latter was firmly established as the voice of the Baltimore Bullets' National Basketball Association team and had built a substantial following in that role. According to Costello, shifting to baseball announcing would be a "piece of cake" for Karvellas. Those attending the meeting with Costello were Hoffberger, Cashen, Bride, and Harry Dalton.

When Karvellas' name was brought up, Dalton interrupted Costello. Harry said, "Wait a minute! There's a broadcaster on our top farm club, Rochester, who does a tremendous job of play-by-play, Joe Cullinane. Besides, he knows our ball club as well as anyone."

To placate the group, Costello agreed to a series of on-air auditions. I had been warned in Miami by Frank Lane and others that Costello and Karvellas were extremely close, frequently socializing together. I was later told by several people close to the scene that the so-called auditions were completely phony, a veritable smoke screen. Costello, bestowed with total power to select the new announcer without interference, planned from the beginning to install Karvellas.

One might wonder why Cashen, who professed a strong liking for my work, didn't overrule Costello. There was a reason. Years earlier, Cashen and Costello had worked together as Life magazine writers. When Cashen left Life, he joined National Brewing Company as advertising director. When Frank became an Orioles' vice president, he was reluctant to veto his successor's decision.

CHAPTER 15: MY BIG CHANCE

Even after hearing Joe Bride's detailed story, it still seemed strange to me that the Orioles allowed Costello to conduct what essentially proved to be bogus on-air auditions. Why did they allow me to entertain high hopes? They could easily have sent me a simple rejection letter. Earl Weaver, ever a loyal friend, even went to Hoffberger on my behalf, but the owner told Earl he wouldn't interfere with Costello's decision. When the Orioles came to Rochester for a June exhibition game, Weaver, stepping off the plane, inquired, "Are you down?" It was the sharp dip of the roller coaster.

I felt an anger difficult to dismiss. Baltimore trainer Ralph Salvon told me essentially I was robbed, although he expressed that idea in much stronger, earthy terms. Baltimore sports writers John Steadman and Neal Eskridge, also expressed strong opinions that I had been the recipient of shabby treatment. Adding to the irony, had I latched onto the Orioles' assignment, I would also have become radio voice of the Baltimore Colts, who that season would advance to the Super Bowl before bowing to Joe Namath and the New York Jets.

And what became of Karvellas? He was fired after two seasons, proof positive that one's basketball announcing ability doesn't necessarily mean that talent can be duplicated in baseball broadcasting. Costello, imposing title notwithstanding, proved he was ill-equipped to select a baseball broadcaster.

In subsequent years, while still in Baltimore and before he became New York Mets' general manager, Cashen frequently called or wrote me in Rochester, ever willing to recommend me should big league broadcasting opportunities develop elsewhere. But as one Rochesterian cynically observed: "What credibility would a Cashen recommendation have? The Orioles had their own perfect chance to hire you and blew it."

16 PICKING UP THE PIECES

After my Baltimore dream was shattered, I buried myself in the task of covering the 1968 Red Wings, managed by former big league infielder Billy DeMars. Not as stormy or loquacious as Earl Weaver, DeMars was still a stern taskmaster. Like Weaver, he had worked and clawed his way up through the Orioles' system. DeMars left no doubt about who was in charge. Discipline and precise execution of fundamentals were almost an extension of his personality. Billy put together a very competitive team.

Third baseman/outfielder, Bill Scripture, was so strong he could break a bat in two pieces with his hands. Also, he would literally take a bite out of a baseball, much to the disapproval of his dentist. Only 5'8", he weighed approximately 185 pounds and possessed phenomenal strength. Once, summoned to pinch hit, he confidently informed his teammates, "Bag up the balls, fellas, I'm goin' downtown." Then he proceeded to wallop a tape measure, game-winning home run.

Center fielder, Merv Rettenmund, had an amazing year. He had been a standout running back at Ball State College and the Dallas Cowboys wanted him. But Rettenmund opted for baseball and swiftly reached the triple A level. He possessed impressive tools. His outstanding speed, unusual for an athlete with a muscular, blocky physique, enabled him to cover vast acreage in center field; all-important in that huge area of the Rochester ballpark. That alone would have made him a standout, but he also brought impressive power and hitting consistency. The Orioles' hierarchy insisted that DeMars provide Rettenmund with as many at bats as possible, even if it meant sacrificing much of his RBI potential.

Billy installed Rettenmund in the leadoff spot and that's where he remained. Ever hear of a leadoff man who led his team in home runs? That's exactly what Rettenmund accomplished. Astoundingly, he led the team in every offensive category: homers, triples, doubles, singles, total hits, walks, runs scored, RBIs, plate appearances, and batting average. There's no telling how many runs Rettenmund would have driven across had he batted in a power hitter's more customary positions in the batting order; third, fourth or fifth.

I never saw a leadoff batter quite like Merv Rettenmund. Before a game in Niagara Falls, transplanted home of the Buffalo Bisons, I told my listeners that home runs to Hyde Park Stadium's left field would be at a premium.

The distance from home plate to the left field foul pole was measured at an extremely deep 360 feet. That was longer than in any major league ballpark. Rettenmund promptly made my prediction appear foolish. All he did, leading off, was to blast TWO HOME RUNS IN THE FIRST INNING (both to left field)! He was making a joke of the game.

There came a point in the season when Baltimore, which had replaced Hank Bauer as manager with Earl

Weaver, made a strong but unsuccessful run trying to overhaul the pennant-bound Detroit Tigers. To bolster their already productive attack, the Orioles summoned Rettenmund from Rochester. Merv quickly demonstrated he belonged on a major league team.

The Orioles had a bright young prospect who had produced an outstanding season in the Class C California League with Stockton. He was fleet footed and a power-hitting 19-year-old outfielder named, Don Baylor. Late in the season, Baylor was elevated over two classifications, B and A, and ordered to report to the Orioles' Class Double A Elmira affiliate, located on New York state's southern tier.

Baylor was hardly there long enough to unpack his bags when he was ordered to Rochester as Rettenmund's center field replacement. Thrust into the lineup immediately, Baylor was at an immediate disadvantage covering the sprawling center field acreage. He had injured his arm and shoulder playing high school football in Austin, Texas. Throughout his career he found it difficult to make long, hard throws. Additionally, Triple A pitching, at times, ate him up and during a six-week stay in Rochester, he batted just .246. That still wasn't bad for a player leap-frogging over three classifications to take on the difficult job of playing in a league one short step from the majors. He was vulnerable and at the mercy of crafty pitchers fully aware of how to change speeds to keep a hitter off balance and how to induce eager young batters into swinging at pitches well removed from the strike zone. Baylor was an aggressive base runner and fearlessly stood in against all pitchers. That would become one of his trademarks in a long and successful big league career.

There was one ugly incident that marred the 1968 campaign. Jim Palmer, unable to shake persistent arm trouble, again was sent down to the Red Wings by Baltimore. Still only 22, Jim was an unsightly mess on the mound. He had lost his rhythm, his consistency and there was hardly a semblance of his once sharp control.

I doubt whether DeMars wanted Palmer on his ball club. One Sunday, pitching before a sizeable gathering of Red Wing fans, Palmer was his typically ineffective self. At times he appeared to be shotputting the ball toward home plate. What a contrast to the smooth, flawless, straight over-the-top delivery we all would come to know so well and appreciate. When DeMars strode briskly to the mound to remove Palmer, Jim threw a temper tantrum. He angrily flipped the ball to his equally upset manager, then stormed off the diamond.

When I paid a post-game visit to the clubhouse, I was near Palmer's locker when I heard an angry-voiced DeMars in his office bellowing to Baltimore's regional scouting director, Frank McGowan, "I don't want Palmer on my ball club. The kid is gutless."

A distraught Palmer had to have heard it, too. The upshot was that Jim was again banished to Elmira, just as he had been in 1967. I felt downright sad about it, for I truly liked Jim. When Palmer couldn't produce for Elmira, he was sent further down the ladder, descending all the way to Miami of the Class A Florida State League. The Orioles were hoping the combination of heat and humidity would put minimal strain of Jim's ailing arm.

CHAPTER 16: PICKING UP THE PIECES

When Palmer was demoted in 1968, who could have envisioned he would one day again become a World Series hero, a Hall of Famer, a TV baseball analyst, a successful television commercial pitch man, and a very recognizable model of men's underwear? Years later, when I taped an interview with him in Denver, I found him unchanged from the Jim Palmer I knew and liked so well.

Just about everything was tried in a seemingly futile attempt to restore Jim to the pitcher he had been while winning fifteen games and hurling a World Series shutout barely two years earlier at the age of 20. What finally enabled him to get back on track was a simple shoe lift that somehow took the strain off his arm. By 1969 he was back all the way, en route to his fabulous Hall of Fame career.

DeMars' Red Wings advanced to the playoffs in 1968 and were eliminated in the first round. Billy was then hired by Bob Skinner as the Phillies' batting coach.

Hank Bauer managed Tidewater in the playoffs that year against Rochester. The parent club of the New York Mets had offered him the job after his firing in Baltimore. After a playoff game in Rochester, Bauer requested I chauffeur him to his downtown hotel. When we emerged from the clubhouse, there were only two remaining cars in the parking lot. Bauer headed for a Buick before I halted him in his tracks, hollering, "No, Hank. You've got the wrong car."

Heading for my Volkswagen bug, Bauer growled, "Dammit, Joe. Is that the best you can do?"

I replied, "Just a minute, Hank. Take a look at that sign." Atop my vehicle was an advertisement by the car dealer who sponsored my post game program, "Here comes Joe."

I can assure you Hank was duly impressed, particularly when I informed him the car was GIVEN to me for the season. Hank would have been even more impressed if he had known about the OTHER car furnished to me by a radio sponsor. It was a Cadillac, complete with stereo system. Following my sponsors' wishes, I alternated driving the two vehicles during the season.

During my thirteen years in Rochester there were six managers. Five became big league pilots, three led teams into the World Series, including four times by Weaver. Billy DeMars reached the majors as a coach, first with Philadelphia, then with Cincinnati. That made a strong statement for the Orioles' system and their unwavering stress on teaching fundamentals. DeMars gained a well deserved reputation as one of baseball's foremost hitting instructors, before Marge Schott's meddling in Cincinnati so disgusted him that he quit the game.

DeMars' successor as Red Wing skipper was Cal Ripken, father of Baltimore's iron man All-Star shortstop. Like predecessors Weaver and DeMars, Ripken nurtured his managerial skills in the Orioles' model farm system. I still remember, long after Red Wings' games in 1969 and '70, two little boys playing catch in Rochester's dimly lit parking lot. Occasionally an errant throw would bounce off my car.

Then the boys' mother would warn them, "Now Calvin and Billy, you stop that." Little did I suspect they would one day form a double play combination for the Orioles, Cal Jr. and Billy Ripken.

The A. Rae Hickok awards banquet in Rochester was held in January of 1969. It was America's most prestigious

CHAPTER 16: PICKING UP THE PIECES

sports banquet. "The Dinner," as it was known, honored the nation's professional sports athlete of the year. The coveted prize was the Hickok Belt, emblematic of supremacy among all pro athletes. The diamond-studded belt was worth a minimum of $10,000. Plus there were lucrative endorsements that would automatically open up for the winner.

The previous season produced baseball's first thirty game winner in 34 years. Denny McLain, the Detroit Tigers' hurler who spearheaded his team's ascension to the throne in 1968, chalked up a startling 31-6 regular season record.

McLain arrived in Rochester, along with pitching teammate Mickey Lolich. The rotund Lolich had won three World Series games against the Cardinals and the indomitable Bob Gibson. It appeared that Denny was a cinch to win the coveted Hickok Belt. Many in the vast audience were astounded when the winner was announced. It was Joe Namath, quarterback of the New York Jets football team and the principal architect of the Jets' stunning Super Bowl upheaval of the heavily favored Baltimore Colts.

Following the announcement, Lolich and McLain were both called upon to speak. McLain graciously congratulated Namath. Lolich was another matter. He proceeded to insult the voters, whose ranks included a sizeable contingent of New York City sportswriters. Lolich didn't stop there. He rudely insulted the event's sponsor, A. Rae Hickok, who was visibly angry and mortified by Lolich's boorish outburst. After concluding his tirade, Lolich made the whole scene even more outrageous by storming out of the banquet room right in the middle of the festivities.

McLain couldn't have been more gracious. He even refused to accept expenses for flying to Rochester for the charity affair. I suspected Lolich might have been acting out of character. Maybe things would have turned out better had Lolich not attended the pre-banquet cocktail bash.

Don Baylor didn't come back to Rochester in 1969. The Orioles characteristically avoided rushing their farmhands. Don spent that entire season at Dallas-Ft. Worth of the Double A Texas League, under the tutelage of Joe Altobelli.

Altobelli managed Baylor at every minor league way station beginning with the rookie league in Bluefield, West Virginia then onto Stockton of the California League. A year of grooming in the Texas League was followed by two full seasons in Rochester, where he was selected minor league Player-of-the-Year in 1970. There's no denying Baylor had a valuable apprenticeship before launching a lengthy and brilliant major league career. I don't think baseball will ever again see one manager guiding a player at every step of a slow but steady rise through the minors. Don admitted to me that it was a huge advantage for him to be tutored by a man who had earned a reputation for being an outstanding instructor.

Altobelli, who managed the San Francisco Giants before piloting Baltimore to the World Series championship as Weaver's successor in 1983, is out of uniform these days. He became Red Wings' general manager in his adopted hometown of Rochester, then in 1995 relinquished that assignment.

I well remember when Weaver released Altobelli during the 1966 season. The Orioles' Harry Dalton persuaded Altobelli to begin his managerial career by handling the

CHAPTER 16: PICKING UP THE PIECES

rookie team in Bluefield. Joe's wife, Pat, was hardly overjoyed because a few weeks later she would give birth to their sixth child. She was understandably upset when I talked to her over the phone at the time Altobelli left Rochester.

Despite the presence of sluggers like Roger Freed and Terry Crowley, the Red Wings fell short of reaching the playoffs in 1969; losing out on the final day. That old bugaboo, insufficient pitching depth, did them in.

Ripken returned in 1970 to lead his team into postseason competition. They had a wrecking crew which produced runs in wholesale bunches. Freed was back, along with Bobby Grich and Baylor, now a confident, mature hitter. They punished opposing pitching staffs with many a drive up against or over distant barriers. Grich hit an astonishing .383 before being summoned briefly to Baltimore, en route to another American League title.

The Red Wings again lost out in the first round of playoffs. Hulking reliever, Al Severinson, later to hurl for Baltimore and San Diego, failed to protect an apparently safe lead in the final inning against Columbus. In the clubhouse after the swan song Severinson was shedding copious tears, tormenting himself with second-guessing.

What can an announcer say to an athlete in a revealing moment when he has to come to terms with bitter defeat? Not much. I reminded Al that the Red Wings never would have made the playoffs without his important contributions.

One International League manager of whom I have particularly fond memories was Don Hoak. Hoak, an exboxer and fierce competitor on the diamond, was married to popular recording artist Jill Corey and introduced me to the lovely lady.

Hoak was Pittsburgh's third baseman in the 1960 march to the World Series title, when Bill Mazeroski belted his historic series-ending home run. When he managed the Columbus Jets, Hoak removed center fielder John Jeter in the middle of an inning, openly embarrassing the proud and talented player. Jeter hadn't hustled after a ball to Hoak's satisfaction.

When I asked Hoak about the incident, he snapped, "Nobody plays for Don Hoak unless he breaks his rear end."

Hoak fervently wanted to manage the Pirates and made no secret of his desire. Shortly after he was bypassed, he suffered a fatal heart attack. I've always suspected there was a connection.

The 1970 season marked the last of Cal Ripken as Rochester manager. He was reassigned in the Orioles' system, ultimately making it to the majors as Baltimore manager, only to be fired six games into his second season, succeeded by Frank Robinson. That was the year in which a hapless Orioles team lost its first TWENTY-ONE games!

17 SOJOURN IN THE SUN

When the 1969 World Series opened in Baltimore, I was broadcasting the Syracuse-Maryland football game in nearby College Park. I stayed over the following day to tape interviews at Baltimore's Memorial Stadium. I happened to come across Orioles broadcaster, Bill O'Donnell. He asked me whether I'd be going to New York for games three through five. I told him I couldn't, I had other commitments in Rochester. Bill was very persuasive telling me he could get me game tickets and credentials to go onto the field and into the dugouts and clubhouses. I would even be entitled to visit World Series hospitality headquarters at the Americana Hotel before and after games. I would have to arrange and pay for my own transportation to and from New York City. And I would need to find a hotel. Some friends thought that would be difficult to do on short notice.

"What the hell," I told myself. "Postpone your Rochester commitments and take off for New York." Surely I could locate a hotel room after I got there. That's what I did the day prior to game three and the Mets' first World Series appearance ever at Shea Stadium.

I found a hotel room, a flop house if ever I saw one. I had to walk about 100 feet just to take a shower and there were numerous holes in the blankets and sheets. I took every precaution to prevent my tape recorder and other material from being stolen in the night. One couldn't be blamed for wondering whether the cockroaches and other creatures had had to pay as much as I did for my room.

My room cost $3.00 per night, which was about $2.50 too much. There I was, for 3 1/2 days going back and forth between squalor flats and the beautiful Americana Hotel to break bread and visit with many of the sport's luminaries. Former Yankee, Lefty Gomez, invited me to dinner. He was a brilliant pitcher in the thirties. One season he posted a record of 28-5 and he established a still-standing World Series pitching mark of 6-0.

I first met Gomez when he was a good will ambassador for Wilson Sporting Goods. I did many an interview with "El Goofo". He would often sit in with me during broadcasts from Rochester and Syracuse. What a genial companion with a lot of hilarious stories to relate. Gomez was an early roommate of the sometimes somber DiMaggio and must have done much to lighten up Joe's serious approach to life.

When I ventured into the Mets' dugout prior to their first-ever World Series home game, I spotted coach, Joe Pignatano, whose games I announced when he was a Rochester catcher in the early sixties. "Piggy" introduced me to manager, Gil Hodges, and to the likeable Yogi Berra. Both were gracious toward me when I interviewed them. I also talked to several players I had known when they were Mets' farmhands in the International League, slick-fielding shortstop, Bud Harrelson, and pitching standout, Tom Seaver. I reminded Seaver I had announced his first game in organized baseball, but didn't witness the contest. It was a studio re-creation of a Rochester-Jacksonville game. Seaver remembered winning the game and proudly recalled whacking a double. Like most pitchers, Seaver relished swinging the bat.

It was an unforgettable Series. Baltimore had been established as the heavy favorite. In retrospect, I wondered why the Orioles were thought to be superior to the New York upstarts. After all, the Mets had overcome a seemingly insurmountable lead to overhaul Leo Durocher's powerful Cubs, a hitting machine, led by Ernie Banks, Billy Williams, and Ron Santo. The Mets had gotten superb pitching from Seaver, Jerry Koosman, Gary Gentry, and bullpen-stopper, Tug McGraw. They were an average offensive ball club, but got important clutch hitting from Cleon Jones and Don Clendenon. Taking full advantage of his versatile roster, Hodges platooned at five positions. Only Casey Stengel's Yankees ever resorted to such wide-scale platooning as much as the stern, but soft-spoken Hodges.

I moved into the Orioles' dugout before game three, as sullen skies hovered over the big stadium in Queens. My old friend, Earl Weaver, was tense and cranky. The cocky bantering wasn't in evidence. Perhaps even then, with the Classic deadlocked at one game apiece, Earl had a premonition of the disaster about to befall his team. I didn't notice a similar nervousness among other Orioles I interviewed. Veterans like Frank and Brooks Robinson, Don Buford and the always confident Dave McNally. Jim Palmer, who had come back so far in such a short time, was there too. They all appeared calm and relaxed.

So many emotions manifest themselves in the pressure cooker that is the World Series. There is, for some players, shivering excitement as zero hour approaches. Others, like jovial, easy going, Boog Powell, are blessed with the temperament to relax. They just go out and play ball, reveling in the glaring spotlight. Sometimes you can look into a player's eyes and determine his mood.

I've often felt that players and managers' thinking powers occasionally desert them in the fury of a World Series. A case in point was Earl Weaver who was ejected by umpire, Shag Crawford, after an altercation during game four. Earl designated third base coach Bill Hunter to take over the reins.

In the ninth inning, with score tied and bedlam prevailing at Shea Stadium, Pete Richert came in to relieve for the Orioles. With pinch-runner, Rod Gaspar, at first base, J.C. Martin stepped in against Richert. Martin dropped a bunt down the first base line. Southpaw Richert moved quickly to field the ball, spun into throwing position and fired toward first base. His throw struck Martin in the back, the ball caromed away and Gaspar streaked all the way around from first base to score the winning run. Martin had clearly run out of the basepath, the replays showed. Yet Hunter didn't protest the umpire's non-call in what I've always contended was the key play of the Series. The victory gave the Mets a 3-1 Series edge.

I visited briefly with Hunter that evening and he voiced no explanation as to why he didn't protest. I have great respect for Hunter. He was a strong candidate to replace Hank

Bauer before Weaver was named Hank's successor. Billy later went on to manage the Texas Rangers. The first base umpire was clearly wrong in not calling Martin out. I was looking for Hunter to explode in someone's face.

The Mets were so scorching hot in the last seven weeks of their "miracle" season they had no fear of the more seasoned Orioles. New York used phenomenal pitching as a springboard to winning the world crown in five games.

Both Orioles and Mets had productive farm systems in the years before they clashed in the Series. Both fielded teams in the International League. I had seen these stars in earlier years, while broadcasting their games as they honed their skills. That sort of continuity, step-by- slow-step through the minors, then remaining together as big league teammates would not be found today.

I was fortunate to be in Baltimore at the 1970 World Series when the Orioles dismantled Cincinnati's "Big Red Machine" in five games. Seated alongside me during game five was Rex Barney, the former Brooklyn Dodgers' fireballer. Barney could throw a baseball at 100 mph, but never achieved vital control. Jackie Robinson once told me Barney could stand on the sidelines and fire 15 consecutive strikes but just couldn't do it consistently in game competition.

When Orioles' starting pitcher, Mike Cuellar, encountered typical first inning difficulties, Barney confidently predicted "Crazy Horse" would be in command the remainder of the game. Sure enough, Cuellar completely shut down the Reds with some noticeable assistance from the acrobatic Brooks Robinson. Robinson told me later that it might be impossible for any third baseman today to duplicate that level of fielding wizardry throughout a World Series for one simple reason; odds would be prohibitive against that many balls being hit in a player's direction.

Baltimore won in five games, vindicating the 1969 humiliation at the hands of the upstart Mets. Not to dim the Orioles' luster, but Cincinnati was at a distinct disadvantage. Their pitching ace, Wayne Simpson, was incapacitated by a sore arm. Another mound mainstay, Jim Merritt, was similarly troubled but did pitch. He was ineffective. Reds manager, Sparky Anderson, simply didn't have a full roster.

Orioles' outfielder, Merv Rettenmund, related an amusing story surrounding game four. Rettenmund, not in the Birds' lineup, ventured into Weaver's clubhouse office to watch the final inning and post game wrap-up on television, propping his feet on the manager's desk. Baltimore had appeared to be on the threshold of a sweep until Cincinnati's Lee May blasted a three-run homerun.

Rettenmund should not have been surprised that Earl would be steaming when he stormed into his clubhouse office. Earl demanded in rather crude fashion that Rettenmund leave his office. But the doughty skipper had this parting shot for Merv, "Get ready. You're in there tomorrow." It was a great thrill watching Rettenmund blast an opposite field homerun in the Orioles' clinching triumph.

The first World Series I ever saw, in 1966, was memorable. It was the first World Series ever played in Baltimore. I thought that of all the millions who had played baseball, all the way back to Little League and sandlot days, these were the 18 survivors. I had spent countless hours travelling, interviewing, and sharing meals with four players who trotted onto the field that day to a thunderous ovation. I shared the excitement of Andy Etchebarren, Paul Blair, Curt Blefary, and Dave Johnson. Blefary was so nervous during the 1966 Series that his entire body broke out in hives.

I was the last announcer to interview Dodger Manager, Walt Alston, before the final game of the 1966 World Series. Half an hour before the start of a World Series game, all media personnel are required to leave the dugouts. About 20 minutes before the first pitch, I was still near the Los Angeles dugout when I spotted Alston standing alone. Walt had once played for the Red Wings. I told the security guard I needed to have a few words with the Los Angeles skipper and Walt nodded. I don't normally bother athletes or managers that close to zero hour, but it was a special situation that worked out. I had nothing to lose, even had I been turned away. Alston was very accommodating, answering all my questions.

From the early to mid-sixties, baseball's most dominant pitcher was Sandy Koufax, the brilliant Los Angeles Dodgers' southpaw. Four no-hitters, high strikeout totals, the incredible won-lost percentages, and Sandy's miniscule earned run averages made Koufax "King of the Hill." All Sandy lacked was longevity. When he first joined the Dodgers, his sheer stuff was unbelievable. He could fire his fast ball through the proverbial brick wall and his sharp-breaking overhand curve would often drop a foot. In Koufax's heyday, even great hitters were over-matched. The most appropriate description of his pitching could be summed up in one word: unhittable.

But in the early years, Sandy couldn't throw strikes consistently enough to fully exploit that great arm. Keen-eyed observers would comment, "If only he had control." Coach Norm Sherry suggested, "Sandy, why don't you make your motion more compact so you can stay within yourself? And why not take a little off your fast ball? You could still overpower hitters and you'd throw a lot more strikes. Give it a try."

Koufax, at the crossroads of his career, responded enthusiastically and, presto, he began to zero in on the strike zone. Never again was control a problem. Koufax was the man who led the light-hitting Dodgers to World Series championships in 1963 and 1965. Sandy and Don Drysdale also pitched the anemic-hitting Dodgers into the 1966 World Series, when the Orioles swept them.

I first met Sandy when he came to Rochester in the mid-sixties to accept the Hickok Belt award as professional athlete-of-the-year. He was most gracious when I interviewed him. He was bright, enthusiastic, insightful and completely at ease. I mention this because after Koufax became a "Game of the Week" network television analyst, by his own admission, he never felt comfortable in the role. He voluntarily resigned that NBC assignment. It was further proof that initiating the conversation can be considerably more difficult than merely responding to questions.

The last time I saw Koufax was when I asked him for an interview during the 1966 Series in Baltimore. Sandy, polite as always, declined, saying, "I've got to do my running now. I'd be happy to do one with you tomorrow."

However, tomorrow never came. The Dodgers and Don Drysdale lost to Baltimore that day and the series was abruptly over. Koufax, suffering from acute pain in his left elbow, never threw another pitch. Several weeks later, he announced his retirement.

Despite winning the '66 series and playing in three straight from 1969 through 1971, Baltimore did not at that time support its great ball clubs in a manner commensurate with the team's success. For the title-clincher in 1970, there were over 5,000 empty seats in Memorial Stadium.

If ever I had an assignment other than play-by-play that was truly exciting, it was doing a program called "The Sounds of the World Series." I did hours of interviews during the '66 Series that were condensed into a half-hour program. Those conversations reflected the confidence of Frank Robinson, the determination of Andy Etchebarren, the nervousness of Curt Blefary, and the happiness of Boog Powell. My lead going into the interviews was "These are the Sounds of the World Series. Certainly, sounds I'll never forget.

18 CHARLIE O.

I met Oakland A's owner, Charlie Finley, at the 1966 World Series in Baltimore and we kept in touch. Finley had a reputation as a man who would diligently pick the brains of dozens of baseball people, trying to gather information about players he wanted to acquire. I can certainly vouch for that. Charlie frequently called my home in Rochester to solicit opinions of Red Wing players like Mike Epstein and Dave Leonhard. (Epstein later played on one of Finley's great World Series teams.) Leonhard made it to Baltimore. After Rochester's season ended in 1969, I called Finley at his Chicago insurance office. Charlie frequently answered his own phone.

Hardly taking time to exchange pleasantries, he practically demanded, "When can you come to Oakland?"

Since the first-ever league championship series was about to start, with the World Series to follow, I suggested, "How about three weeks from now?"

He rapidly countered, "How about three days from now?" Charlie told me he was planning to replace veteran announcer,

Al Helfer, and wanted to give me top consideration. Finley agreed to pay my expenses to Oakland.

I arrived in the San Francisco Bay Area in the wee hours on the day of my scheduled rendezvous with the eccentric Charlie. When I contacted him later that morning, he said he was meeting with General Manager, Phil Seghi, and special instructor, Joe DiMaggio, so he wouldn't be able to see me until that evening. He informed me that his lead announcer, Monte Moore, would be waiting for me at the Oakland Alameda County Coliseum.

The controversial Moore had a reputation of not being the easiest announcer with whom to work. However, Monte and I seemed to hit it off well. He first gave me a tour of the massive gray Coliseum, then we met for lunch with executives from the radio station which carried A's games. The meeting went well and by the time Monte dropped me off at my hotel we had spent six pleasant hours together.

After leaving Moore, I digested startling news. The San Francisco Examiner's "Green Sheet" (the sports section) reported that Harry Caray had been fired by the St. Louis Cardinals after 25 years. Caray was pictured on the front page of a St. Louis newspaper defiantly quaffing a bottle of Falstaff Beer, a serious competitor of Budweiser. Harry was not adverse to burning bridges.

I met Finley, accompanied by his cousin Carl, at the Elegant Farmer Restaurant in Jack London Square, an Oakland landmark. Charlie treated me to a great meal and then the questioning commenced in earnest. At times, it was like an inquisition. He kept asking me, "How did you get along with Monte? What did you talk about?"

CHAPTER 18: CHARLIE O.

I tried to answer his questions patiently, but once I told him, "You already asked me that." He seemed to take it in good grace. In fact, Moore and I had several mutual friends and we found conversation to be relaxed and easy.

Finley eventually got around to asking me whether I had heard the news about Caray's dismissal in St. Louis. I told him I was aware of it. Finley freely admitted he would go after Caray and his exciting voice, but if they didn't make a deal he wanted to give me the opportunity of joining his broadcasting team.

A few days following my return to Rochester, there came a check in the familiar green and gold colors covering the full cost of my trip to Oakland. Only a week later, at the 1969 World Series at Shea Stadium, who do I see sitting in the stands before a game but the irrepressible Caray. Seemingly oblivious to fans sitting around him, Harry loudly questioned me, "Did you see what those suns-uh-bitches did to me?"

While in New York, I read a story that Caray and the Cincinnati Reds were having "serious conversations." You can bet I rooted hard for Harry. Nothing materialized and the next thing I knew, Harry went to Oakland to broadcast A's games. He lasted one year before moving to Chicago to take over broadcasts of White Sox' games. Years later, Harry told me he had no problem working for Finley, but found it difficult to co-exist with Monte Moore.

To this day, I still have warm memories of Finley, a man who repeatedly antagonized players, managers and, in particular, rival owners.

Pitcher, Darold Knowles, told me about an unusual contract he had with Charlie Finley. After the usual amount of bickering, the two finally settled on a figure with one important provision. Knowles insisted Charlie include a horse in the deal. Charlie agreed. It's a good thing Knowles didn't request that Finley include the mule, Charlie O. in the transaction.

Finley had one annoying habit he never relinquished. He would call his employees at all hours. Eddie Lopat, for a time the A's general manager, finally found a solution to those sleep interrupting, senseless phone calls. He turned the tables by subjecting his employer to the same treatment. Finley wasn't too pleased, but Lopat told me that henceforth calls from Charlie came only at reasonable hours.

Charlie delighted in harassing Commissioner, Bowie Kuhn, at every opportunity. Who but Charlie would have had the audacity to publicly ridicule the commissioner by referring to Bowie as the "Village Idiot?" Charlie remained bitter toward Kuhn for blocking the sale of high-priced A's players like Joe Rudi, Rick Monday and Bert Campaneris. For the financially strapped Finley, that marked the beginning of the end.

Finley was at his mirthful best playing host to baseball's bigwigs in Oakland's World Series' hospitality room. A close friend of mine, Rochester sports columnist Craig Stolze, was witness to the hilarity. Finley allowed his mule, Charlie O., to circulate freely at these autumn gatherings. Charlie delighted in seeing his favorite mascot eat off the plates of some startled owners with whom Charlie didn't exactly enjoy an abiding friendship. Miss Manners most certainly wouldn't have approved.

Hank Bauer could tell stories about Charlie Finley far into the night. Despite being fired by Charlie, Hank often exclaimed, "Charlie ain't all bad."

Finley had a habit of visiting his team's clubhouse unannounced. Once Charlie frowned while noticing Bauer's uniform. Complained Charlie, "You better change your uniform, Hank. It looks terrible. What's that on the seat of your pants? Are those grass stains?"

Quick on the uptake, Bauer sassed back, "No, Charlie, those aren't grass stains. You're looking at mistletoe."

Hank added that he resigned the Oakland manager's job before Finley could fire him, as Charlie did earlier in Kansas City.

Finley was always helpful to me. Harry Craft, who managed both Houston and Kansas City after playing with championship Cincinnati Reds teams in 1939 and 1940, was also willing to assist me in my quest for a big league announcing job. He voluntarily circulated in the World Series hospitality rooms to locate people he thought might be able to help me.

One very decent and understanding owner was the Minnesota Twins', Calvin Griffith. General managers like Roland Hemond and Lee MacPhail were always considerate. Bob Howsam was consistently approachable and that included the years when he climbed to baseball's pinnacle as the architect of Cincinnati's Big Red Machine. I still visit frequently with Bob. John McHale, Jim Fanning, and Bob Gebhard were Montreal executives who always rolled out a red carpet for me.

Bing Devine was wonderful to me. Buddy Blattner told me that on the day of the seventh World Series game in St.

Louis in 1968, Bing took precious time to talk with Blattner about me. Bing had heard my broadcasts during Rochester visits and strongly recommended me to become Buddy's first broadcast partner in Kansas City when the Royals' became an expansion franchise. That Kansas City chose a local voice, Denny Matthews, was beside the point. Devine was a loyal friend.

As always, baseball was not my only sport. I broadcast a huge number of basketball games in Rochester, both college and high school. Les Harrison, who coached the Rochester Royals to the 1950 NBA championship, overcoming the New York Knicks in the finals, would frequently serve as analyst. He had a colorful delivery and was adept at dissecting the action. I was miffed when Rochester basketball coach, Lyle Brown, informed me some English professors complained that Harrison's grammar was atrocious. They suggested he be removed from the broadcasts. I told Lyle those stuffed shirts had best retreat to their ivory towers.

Even after the Royals' franchise moved to Cincinnati, thousands of Rochester fans remained close followers of the NBA. Harrison promoted a regular league game at Rochester War Memorial Auditorium. The arena was filled as Rochesterians welcomed the Royals back to their former home. I handled the public address announcing and checked both rosters carefully long before the game. One player's name and number was inserted in the middle of the Cincinnati roster. I decided that wouldn't do, that we needed to make that player the final one introduced. The auditorium was darkened and a spotlight followed each player to midcourt as I introduced starting lineups.

CHAPTER 18: CHARLIE O.

Falsely assuming I had introduced every player, I was in the process of asking the fans to rise for the playing of our National Anthem when suddenly I heard a loud and irate voice, that of the Royals' trainer, berating me. I had FORGOTTEN OSCAR ROBERTSON. I quickly glanced to my right to see a scowling "Big O." I had left one of the sport's premier players standing! There was still time to make amends. Rather than, "Please rise for the playing of Our National Anthem," I merely shifted gears and asked the assemblage to, "Please rise and let's hear a big Rochester welcome for one of the greatest players of all time, the BIG O, Oscar Robertson!"

The University of Rochester basketball play-by-play assignment was one I always enjoyed. They didn't constantly schedule top teams for a very good reason. Like Ivy League schools, Rochester focused on academics. There were no basketball scholarships per se. Recruiters were limited to top students only. Still, the team tackled more than its share of top-flight competition. I broadcast two U of R games against the Cadets of Army, one at West Point. I don't recall a youthful Bobby Knight indiscriminately throwing chairs onto the court.

When playing Fordham, I stayed at the old Concourse Plaza Hotel, across the street from Yankee Stadium. My roommate, sportswriter Dave Warner, couldn't resist cracking, "Babe Ruth slept here and they haven't changed the sheets since then." Fordham's coach was "Digger" Phelps, who went on to later coach at Notre Dame.

Rochester had a gifted shooter named Bill Baum. He was consistently off target against Fordham. From the Rose

Hill campus, I rode back to our hotel after the game with Bill and his parents. His mother asked sweetly, "Where the hell were you tonight, Billy? You didn't get off your dead ass the whole ball game!"

I don't recall Bill's reply, but I wondered what mom might be apt to say if she had even greater reason to be upset.

19 PLEASE PASS THE COUGH SYRUP

On a late December trip to play Stetson University in DeLand and Florida Southern in Lakeland, I came down with a cold, which unfortunately went into laryngitis. In Florida, of all places. I didn't have the luxury of a color man, so I croaked my way through the entire broadcast. When I arrived at home following the trip, my wife's first three words of greeting were, "You sounded awful."

While in Florida, I telephoned Ernie Harwell. He graciously invited me to be his houseguest, but I had to decline due to a tight schedule resulting from my again having to be my own engineer. Ernie suggested I rent a car and meet him halfway between Lakeland and his Gulf Coast home in Dunedin. He was willing to drive a considerable distance in order to visit with me and treat me to a delicious dinner at Al Lopez' Tampa restaurant. I can't recall ever having met a kinder, more gracious gentleman than Ernie Harwell. When Russ Hodges made his wildly excited call of Bobby Thomson's home run off Ralph Branca, Harwell was describing the historic moment on television.

I've always appreciated announcers who develop their own inimitable descriptions. A minor league ball club had a manager who doubled as a pitcher. The skipper was having a difficult time of it one night on the mound. After absorbing a pummeling, he signaled for bullpen help, whereupon the announcer informed his listeners, "Well, whaddya know? There's our good skipper relieving himself right out there in the middle of the diamond."

Ball players can be notorious pranksters. At the Tigers' spring training stomping grounds in Lakeland, Florida, I met a tall Detroit outfielder. I asked him whether he answered to the name of Kirk Gibson.

He replied, "Right on," and cheerfully agreed to be interviewed. In addition to baseball, we delved into his career as a wide receiver at Michigan State. Just as I prepared to wind up the interview, a Tigers' player whispered that his teammates were playing an April Fools' Day joke on me. At that moment the real Kirk Gibson cheerfully introduced himself to me. The pretender was flaky pitcher, Dave Rozema. Gibson quickly consented to speak for himself and made a most interesting guest.

How important is it for a sportscaster to have played? I think it's a significant plus. I played sports as a boy, and as a teenager I played in the well-organized Chicago Baseball Federation. By playing the game, a broadcaster can acquire a feel for the competition.

There's one sport I should have never attempted and that's golf. When I worked in Freeport I was coerced into competing in a tournament. Predictably, having ignored the sport, I shot 179 and took forever to complete 18 holes. When

CHAPTER 19: PLEASE PASS THE COUGH SYRUP

I walked into the station the next day, a huge reception committee greeted me with a loud ovation. They presented me a scroll, tied with a colorful ribbon. I opened the scroll to discover a shining gold tee and an accompanying message: "Have you ever tried croquet?"

As the Rochester Red Wings assembled for the 1971 season, a new manager awaited them. Joe Altobelli, who had played 3-1/2 seasons in his adopted home town, had battled his way to the Triple A manager's job after moving up painstakingly through every classification in the Orioles' minor league system.

Grich and Baylor were returnees despite their phenomenal year in 1970. Now, you'd never see a player returning to the minors after a year similar to what inseparable roommates Grich and Baylor achieved in 1970. There was no room at the top in 1971. Their time, however, would come soon.

Grich was confronted with the reality of a championship Baltimore team that had Mark

Belanger and Dave Johnson functioning superbly as the shortstop/second base combination. Similarly, the Orioles' outfield was already stacked with veterans like Frank Robinson, Paul Blair, Don Buford, and Merv Rettenmund.

Grich and Baylor were leading bulwarks on the pennant winning 1971 Red Wings. That was a unique team. Six position players and five pitchers graduated to the majors the next season. Furthermore, five members eventually became major league managers. There was Altobelli, third baseman Mike Ferraro, catcher Johnny Oates, pitcher Ray Miller and left fielder Baylor. I had never before heard of one minor league team ultimately producing FIVE major league field generals.

    1971 was special in a personal way. Through the years I had journeyed by bus, car, train, commercial airlines, and even via ferry boat across the St. Lawrence River while covering hockey. For baseball we traveled by charter airplane in 1971, to my knowledge the only minor league team ever to enjoy that luxury. It was for that year only; too expensive to continue. It was also the first year I broadcast all games live. No more re-creations!

    Despite their impressive array of talent, the Red Wings got off to a sputtering start in 1971, due principally to acute pitching deficiencies. About three weeks into the season, Rochester acquired a right-handed fireballer named Roric Harrison, who overcame a pronounced tendency toward wildness. In what for him was a shortened season, he chalked up 15 victories. I never saw a pitcher experience a hitting day quite like the one Harrison had against Toledo. While firing a two-hit shutout over the Mudhens, he slammed FOUR doubles and drove across SEVEN runs. The game was played before an embarrassingly sparse Sunday afternoon gathering in the Lucas County Recreation Center. How's that for the name of a ballpark? Harrison, despite my lofty vantage point, told me he could hear me describe every pitch. What an eerie feeling for a pitcher, listening to the description of his own game.

    The 1971 Red Wings were a closely-knit team whose players hit it off unusually well. I remember the entire ball club going into a restaurant adjoining the Charleston, West

CHAPTER 19: PLEASE PASS THE COUGH SYRUP

Virginia ballpark for a pre-game meal. That sort of team unity is non-existent these days in all of professional sports.

Harrison's season came to an abrupt end during the International League playoffs in Syracuse when he badly damaged his ankle sliding into second base, trying to stretch a single into a double. How many pitchers would run bases so aggressively? Rochester summoned Wayne Garland from Double A ball. He delivered a masterful clutch performance to help Rochester win the I.L. playoff finals over Hank Bauer's Tidewater Tides. That qualified the Red Wings to meet the Denver Bears in minor league baseball's Junior World Series.

Because Mile High Stadium was pre-empted by the Denver Broncos, all games were played in Rochester. Denver was designated as the home team for games three, four and five. The Red Wings batted first in those encounters. Rochester was excited about hosting this premier showdown and despite some very uncomfortable September weather, huge numbers of fans flocked into Silver Stadium to witness a series that went the maximum seven games before Rochester prevailed.

A cold rain descended on Rochester the day the Junior World Series opened. So confident was I that the battle would be postponed that I submitted to a tooth extraction. Emerging from the dentist's chair, still numb from a heavy injection of novocaine, I discovered to my consternation that the game was still on!

That wasn't the worst. In May of 1971, I described a game from windswept Winnipeg; the Montreal Expos' International League affiliate. A temporary fence had been erected in left field, but I wondered whether it would remain in place. Sure enough a strong wind gust blew the fence away. I told my listeners the fence would probably come to rest in the adjoining western province of Saskatchewan. Meanwhile, the home plate umpire signaled the press box and radio booth that the game was to be postponed. I informed my listeners, recapped the game to that point, and said what the airtime would be the following day.

You can imagine my surprise when the umpires reappeared about 15 minutes later and made the startling pronouncement that the windblown fence had been retrieved and would be put back in place in order to finish the game. I called Rochester to inform a mystified engineer that we would be resuming the broadcast after all. I was plenty irritated by the illogical decision to play again AFTER my listening audience was essentially lost.

I spent a great deal of time in 1971 with utility infielder, Ron Shelton. He was sidelined for an extended period due to back problems. He would join me in the radio booth in Rochester and on the road, too. In Richmond I practically delivered an ultimatum to Ron that we tour the Edgar Allen Poe Museum. An English major at USC, he was fascinated by the tour as I knew he would be. As we strolled the ancient cobbled walk in the backyard garden, I listened, enraptured, to the soft Southern voice of the tour guide, a woman obviously dedicated to her task.

"This is where Edgah Allin, so 'legind has it, would 'oft-tahms' stroll of a summah' evenin', perhaps composin' some of his immawtul' lahns'." The guide took us to an area where we could read some of Poe's original manuscripts and we ascended a spiral staircase to view magnificent portraits in the "Raven Room." Beneath each portrait was a stanza of the famous, haunting poem. I was glad to know that Shelton was every bit as mesmerized as I was during the tour.

Shelton is now renowned as the writer/director of several successful motion pictures including Bull Durham, White Men Can't Jump, Tin Cup, and Cobb; a sobering film about the brilliant but demonic "Georgia Peach." It has been reported that "Bull Durham" grossed $250 million.

Late in the 1971 season I entered the Rochester clubhouse before a game and was promptly asked to leave because a team meeting was in progress. I thought nothing of it. Weeks later, I read a newspaper story about the Junior World Series. The story included information about how the players' shares were to be divided. I was joyously startled to see my name listed under "half shares." I even remember the exact amount, $569.78. What a totally unexpected windfall! I was later told the reason why I was asked to leave the clubhouse during that 1971 meeting. The whole get-together was about how post season players' shares would be divided.

When I saw both Grich and Baylor in Miami the following spring, they told me several players wanted to award me a full share. However, they didn't wish to offend trainers, equipment managers and others who wouldn't be receiving full amounts. What a magnanimous gesture, a broadcaster being treated just like a player. I don't mind admitting I was deeply touched. I might have been the only announcer ever to have received even a portion of players' post season spoils.

These days in many cities there is a built-in wariness, sometimes a strong antipathy between players and the media. One must earn the players' trust by being fair and evenhanded with one's criticism.

Looking back, not only did the Red Wings vote me a half share of their purse, but that same season the players contributed a substantial sum when the ball club staged a "night" for me. During the 1966 International League playoffs, Rochester shortstop, Mark Belanger, insisted on buying me the "best steak dinner in Richmond" because he had heard I said many complimentary things about him on the air. How could I help but voice compliments about Belanger, the best minor league defensive shortstop I ever saw? There is a marked tendency to attach the word "greedy" to all ball players these days, but there have been many wonderful, generous people among the players I've known.

I never once "shilled" for a player or ball club. I pride myself in giving an accurate account. As for Belanger, I can still visualize his gliding gracefully into the deep hole at short to produce astounding plays. By the same token, if a player delivered a bad or slipshod performance, as all occasionally do, I would tell my audience as much. But I refuse to dwell at length on negatives. That's not what the listening audience wants.

There are announcers who claim they don't even inwardly pull for teams whose games they broadcast, that they announce the games without becoming emotionally involved. I find that difficult to comprehend. I ALWAYS pulled for the teams with whom I was associated without openly rooting for them.

Red Barber was adamant in his belief and practice of not associating with players and managers off the field; fearful it would color his views and adversely affect his accurate reporting. How better to get to know players and managers than to spend plenty of time with them on AND off the field? One can still maintain objectivity while describing games. I totally disagreed with Red.

While covering spring training for Rochester, infielders asked me to hit ground balls to them during batting practice. It's something I never would have the chance to consider, during the regular season.

In the early eighties, the Montreal Expos were winding up spring training for all their minor league farmhands. Camp coordinator Bob Gebhard, a former big league pitcher and former General Manager of the Colorado Rockies, addressed the entire assemblage of players over the loud speaker, "We have in our midst a broadcaster who has second-guessed us all through spring training. It's time to find out about his credibility. Joe Cullinane, grab a bat."

I hadn't swung a bat in earnest for years even though I frequently batted against Bob Feller when he pitched to media members during promotional appearances. Gebhard threw to me for about ten minutes before all those critical onlookers. Afterward, Denver Bears manager, Felipe Alou, told me, "You sure have a SLOW bat."

Hey, my job was to describe base hits…not get them. It was still fun.

20 MANAGER MERRY-GO-ROUND AND A BIG MOVE

The 1972 Rochester baseball season was almost a let down after the ball club had "run the table" the previous year, winning the pennant, Governor's Cup playoffs and Junior World Series crown in an impressive post season sweep.

The Red Wings gained the post-season playoffs but fans treated shortstop Junior Kennedy in cruel and merciless fashion, angrily booing and verbally taunting him. Before Kennedy's arrival, Red Wing fans had enjoyed an exciting run of watching outstanding shortstops including Belanger, Grich, and Bobby Floyd.

Kennedy was unable to cope with the fans' harsh treatment and buckled under the pressure. It's regrettable that he wasn't sent elsewhere to escape the cynical fans' wrath. He eventually rose to the majors, playing for the Cubs and Reds. Long after his Rochester ordeal, Kennedy confided to me that he found Red Wings' fans unbearable. Many other players expressed nothing but fondness and admiration for Rochester fans and their abiding love affair with baseball.

As the years rolled by, Joe Altobelli, now pining for a big league coaching opportunity, continued to be bypassed by Baltimore. I suspected an underlying personality clash existed between Weaver and Altobelli. Finally, Altobelli got his chance in the majors, not as coach but as manager. It came about in unusual circumstances.

Vern Rapp, after guiding the Denver Bears to an American Association pennant and playoff triumph in 1976, verbally agreed to pilot the San Francisco Giants in 1977. I called Rapp to extend congratulations, whereupon he chided me for not being current with swiftly moving developments. I was on target in congratulating Vern on being named a big league skipper but I didn't properly identify his team. Just after Vern accepted the Giants' offer, he received a call from St. Louis, which also wanted him to manage. All the years of waiting in the wings, then two big league managerial offers came almost simultaneously. Such are the fortunes of baseball.

Vern, a St. Louis native, had a strong preference for the Cardinals' assignment. When he notified San Francisco of the Redbirds' offer, the Giants graciously let Rapp off the hook. Some players, notably Ken Reitz, Ted Simmons, and Al Hrabosky, rebelled at Rapp's enforcement of unbending discipline. Cardinal management and ownership caved in to the players and Rapp was handed his walking papers shortly into his second season. This was despite the fact that in 1977 Vern had the Redbirds in the thick of championship contention until late season.

I always had the highest regard for Rapp. His Denver players loved him and I found him a delight. The year he managed the Bears, I seldom travelled with the team but had a post-game program on which I interviewed Vern. When

CHAPTER 20: MANAGER MERRY-GO-ROUND... 189

the team was at home, no problem existed. I buzzed Rapp on his clubhouse phone. When the team was on the road, he had to place the call to me. That sometimes necessitated his climbing to the press box for phone facilities or even waiting in line to use a pay phone. It was hardly an ideal situation because Vern would have preferred to address his troops IMMEDIATELY after the game. But Vern had made a commitment and his inherent loyalty and never-failing dependability meant he completed his calls to me right on time.

When certain media members complain to me about difficulties in dealing with players and/or managers, I'm never reluctant to tell the story of Vern Rapp. Vern later managed the Cincinnati Reds, but after a brief period he was sacrificed in what I construed to be a public relations move that produced Pete Rose as his successor.

Hrabosky, the sinister looking "Mad Hungarian," told me his only quarrel with Rapp stemmed from the manager's insistence that Hrabosky dispense with his mustache and beard. Hrabosky, a fierce competitor, insisted that the facial hair was an essential part of his mound presence. Rapp won.

Vern's dismissal in St. Louis paved the way for Whitey Herzog to take over as dugout boss. Herzog made history by piloting the Red Birds to three World Series appearances in six years. Years later, when Herzog seemingly lost control of his players, he resigned in mid-season. Somehow I felt he deserted a sinking ship. I didn't respect Whitey for that, though I might not have known the full story.

When the Giants named their new manager, they called the obligatory press conference. Inquisitive media eagerly attended in large numbers. All rumors pointed to Rapp as the new skipper. When Altobelli was introduced, startled queries of "Joe who" abounded. Altobelli did well in the Bay Area, leading the team from a long-standing occupancy of the doldrums. Years later, Joe succeeded the legendary Weaver and struck gold his first year in Baltimore, piloting the Orioles to the World Championship in 1983. When Altobelli was fired during the 1985 season, his successor was none other than his predecessor. The irrepressible Weaver forsook retirement to return to the dugout.

In Rochester, my situation deteriorated in the early seventies. It was becoming increasingly difficult to persuade radio stations to deviate from unbending formats in order to carry live sports events. I needed to broadcast football and basketball to augment my summer income. I couldn't make it year-round on what the Red Wings paid me. Every time I asked for a raise, I got the same tiresome response, "It will have to be taken up with the Board of Directors."

Dealing with a multiplicity of sponsors and handling publicity work during the day, it seemed as though the nightly game broadcasts were almost an afterthought whereas they should have been my almost complete focus.

We moved to Denver early in 1975 after thirteen years in Rochester. The man who hired me to work for the Bears, Jim Burris, was cognizant of my radio ambitions and in my first year he teamed me with Steve Shannon in the broadcast booth. Steve was a talented, happy-go-lucky sort who refused to take himself or life too seriously. He was knowledgeable about baseball, had a strong, commanding delivery and eventually landed big league announcing assignments with Kansas City, California, and Milwaukee. Shannon was succeeded by Mark Holtz, my booth partner for five lively, entertaining and, at times, zany years.

Holtz' most talked-about broadcast occurred on Fireworks Night, July 4, 1979. The Bears were a second-division-bound ball club, so the game itself was hardly significant. But Denver's ninth inning rally was something for the ages. They scored nine runs, EIGHT after two outs, in a stunning comeback victory against Omaha. When Jim Cox blasted his late inning three run homer to win it, Mark came completely unglued.

When we were off the air and he had at long last regained a semblance of calm, he unabashedly asked me whether he had made a fool of himself. I told him no, but added, "you had better make sure there will be no encore." His spontaneous outburst of high excitement was completely sincere and everyone knew it. After all, didn't Russ Hodges "lose it" when describing Bobby Thomson's pennant winning home run?

Mark left to become voice of the NBA Dallas Mavericks in their first year of existence. He was then hired by the Texas Rangers to broadcast their games. Jeff Kingery was selected to succeed Mark. He was immediately successful as a Denver Bears' broadcaster. Kingery had a keen understanding of baseball, always prepared diligently, and had an insatiable desire to learn more.

Jeff possessed an easy-to-listen-to upbeat delivery. When we compared notes, we discovered what a small world it truly is. Years apart, of course, we had both gained experience in Pocatello. We had many mutual friends. That Idaho city was also an early stop for Bill O'Donnell, who later became the Baltimore Orioles' and Colts' voice. Yes, the same Bill O'Donnell with whom I teamed up on the Orioles' network during my so-called "tryout" in 1968.

Kingery's first Denver assignment was broadcasting Colorado Buffalos' basketball games. He later distinguished himself as the popular voice of the Denver Nuggets before teaming up with Wayne Hagin to announce Colorado Rockies' baseball games.

I traveled with Jeff to broadcast all games in 1981 and 1982. Denver's 1981 manager was Felipe Alou, in his first season at the Triple A helm. The Bears got away to a stumbling start, but Alou righted the ship and guided it to a strong finish to earn a playoff berth.

Denver thundered through two post game series including seven straight victories over Evansville and Omaha to win the crown. Alou's troops accomplished this feat despite losing mainstays Tim Raines, Jerry Manuel, and Tim Wallach from the 1980 team which, despite its pennant winning success, bowed ignominiously in post-season competition.

In 1983, when the Denver Bears and radio station KOA couldn't agree on terms of contract renewal, KNUS became the team's radio outlet. Kent Derdivanis, whose top assets were a strong voice and abundant animation, became my Bears' broadcasting cohort. Kent had previous experience as TV voice of the Milwaukee Brewers. After leaving Denver, he did cable television of Boston Red Sox games, then later joined the Pittsburgh Pirates' announcing crew. He was the radio voice of the University of Arizona Wildcats, after which he broadcast UCLA football and basketball.

CHAPTER 20: MANAGER MERRY-GO-ROUND...

During my last year of broadcasting Denver Bears' baseball, I felt I had come full circle with regard to announcing partners. My partner was John Rayburn, possessor of a lively, dynamic, and when the situation warranted, exciting voice. Rayburn and I were Peoria contemporaries, albeit not on the same station. John's resume pointed to versatility. For many years in Denver he was a topflight TV news anchor.

When I worked for the Denver Bears and the city understandably entertained major league ambitions after having been thwarted for so long, fans frequently questioned me, "When are we going to get PRO ball?"

I was tempted to respond, "What in the world do you call what we already have? Aren't you aware that Triple A represents a very high caliber of baseball?"

I was always convinced that many Denver area fans were so obsessed by the glorious prospect of major league baseball coming to the Mile High City that for years they deprived themselves of the opportunity to watch very competitive and entertaining minor league baseball.

In 1976 the Bears' outfield was comprised of a quartet that included Andre Dawson, Ellis Valentine, Warren Cromartie, and Gary Roenicke. Even then, I'd have stacked that group with many an existing major league outfield. Or how about Denver's 1980 infield combination of Tim Wallach, Jerry Manuel, Tim Raines, and Dave Hostetler? You could have moved that entire infield to the major leagues and none would have been overmatched. On a given night, when both pitchers were sharp, the difference between the caliber of big league ball and Triple A would hardly be discernible.

The Bears' and Zephyrs' (a new ownership brought on a name change for the franchise) attendance potential was definitely hindered by the fact that in a city which had NFL, NBA and NHL franchises, baseball remained the city's only minor league professional sport. At that level, playing in so vast a Stadium as Mile High actually hurt attendance. Aside from Fireworks Night, Denver's minor league baseball teams would have fared better playing in a stadium with seating capacity in the fifteen to twenty thousand range.

Alou remained with the Montreal organization to manage Indianapolis and Wichita in the American Association. He was sent to the Expos' lower affiliates for a time, eventually returning to the big leagues as a coach. Alou was given the reins as Montreal manager when the Expos didn't respond to the strict discipline and rigid rules imposed by Tom Runnels. Felipe fought heavy odds to become a major league manager at a much more advanced age than most. It was heartwarming to me when this gracious man was a runaway choice as major league manager of the year in 1994.

Alou was wonderfully cooperative. I once took him to Martin Marietta Corporation southwest of Denver for an employees' get-together the day of a Bears' home game. The appearance consumed hours. I'm sure he had plenty to otherwise occupy his attention, yet he was a great hit with his audience and stayed until the last possible minute.

When the Expos and Bears parted company after the 1981 season, it broke a six-year working agreement. Montreal reportedly wanted its players to become accustomed to synthetic turf before graduating to the Canadian metropolis. They moved to Wichita and a ballpark that had a unique playing surface, comprised of an Astroturf infield and a natural grass outfield.

The Texas Rangers became Denver's parent club for the 1982 season. Former Bears' catcher, Rich Donnelly, managed that team. Despite some impressive and experienced talent, the team failed to make the playoffs. Increasingly, I was discovering the importance of team unity and chemistry among players. The Rangers' front office was in turmoil and couldn't settle on a final big league roster. There was a steady interchange of Triple A and major league players. Constant grumbling emanated from demoted players who felt they weren't given sufficient opportunity to prove their mettle at the top.

Another manager for whom I had a high regard was Jack McKeon, the Denver Bears' skipper in 1979. In the years I worked for them, the Denver Bears spread the gospel of baseball in many communities surrounding the Mile High City. I made trips galore with ball players to conduct their clinics. I normally would take a pitcher, catcher, infielder and outfielder. The two-hour clinics always included a question and answer session along with FREE autographs. We would form four groups of boys and girls of all ages and have the players rotate. That way each group would benefit from specific instructions from all four players in every fundamental aspect of the game.

Roger Freed, Al "the Mad Hungarian" Hrabosky, Ron Karkovice, Dave Hostetler, Bill Atkinson, Bob Reece, Dan Briggs, Lamar Johnson and Sam Ewing were outstanding and willing instructors.

Not only would he insist that players attend, but McKeon himself would sometimes lend his expertise. Jack also volunteered anytime I thought his presence would be helpful in making a ticket or program pitch. In addition to broadcasting, I worked in sales and marketing for the Bears as I had in Rochester.

Knowing McKeon's tireless work ethic, I wasn't surprised when Jack wore two hats for the San Diego Padres, general manager and manager. That just isn't done any more in major league baseball. Jack also managed the Kansas City Royals and peripatetic Charlie Finley's Oakland A's as well as the Cincinnati Reds.

21 FROM "THE BULLIES" TO "THE DOCTOR"

In addition to Bears' baseball, I latched onto other engrossing assignments after moving to Denver. Bears' General Manager, Jim Burris, permitted me to freelance as long as it didn't interfere with my sales and public relations commitments. I enjoyed working for Burris. He always rewarded productivity. Bears' owner, Gerry Phipps, who also owned the Broncos for a number of years, once approached my office at Mile High Stadium. Before coming in he asked my PERMISSION. Imagine that, an owner requesting an employee's permission to see him! All he wanted to do was to thank me personally for my contributions and hand me a generous bonus. Burris and Phipps were hardly typical.

During the mid-seventies, Denver was awarded a National Hockey League franchise, called the Rockies. The team was moved from Kansas City where it failed. I was named the team's public address announcer. To this day I'm firmly convinced the fans' support of the club was positive even though the team wasn't competitive and had too many changes of ownership. In retrospect, it's a wonder the Rockies lasted six years in Denver.

Management and ownership made a glaring and inexplicable mistake when Don Cherry was fired following only one season as coach. Cherry came to Denver after a successful stint with the Boston Bruins, twice taking his team to the Stanley Cup finals. The Rockies, far short of being playoff caliber, nevertheless improved markedly under Cherry. Positive fan response was reflected in sharply rising attendance figures. Don, ever a forceful and combative individual, became embroiled with management over how to run the team. Rather than attempting to work out the difficulties; the Rockies took the easy way out. They fired their best public relations asset ever. To many fans, Cherry WAS the franchise.

After Cherry was handed his walking papers, the downward spiral was inevitable. It surprised no one when the franchise was moved to the brand new Brendan Byrne Arena in East Rutherford, New Jersey. Thoroughly disenchanted with fickle ownership, fans angrily responded with, "good riddance."

I vividly recall a visit I had with old Rochester Americans' friend, Al Arbour, when he brought his New York Islanders to Denver for the last time. Al expressed regret that Colorado fans wouldn't support their hockey team. That's when I challenged him to name as many as three American cities that, under similar adverse circumstances, would have supported their team as well. Arbour saw my point but by that time it was too late. The moving vans were all but assembled for the team's departure to the Atlantic Coast.

Denver hockey fans would soon be deprived of watching some of the greatest players in hockey history. Players like swift skating Guy LaFleur of the dynastic Montreal

Canadiens, the fast developing Wayne Gretzky, ageless wonder Gordie Howe and the brilliant defenseman, Barry Beck, once a Colorado player himself.

As public address announcer, I always tried to adopt a mode of strict neutrality. Thus I was understandably flabbergasted when referee Bob Myers skated over to me and complained, "I don't like your voice inflections!" The same Bob Myers later invited me to the officials' dressing room, where we taped an interview. He was refreshingly accommodating.

My seat at old McNichols Arena was situated on the ice. It was necessary because the referee had to explain to the announcer the penalties and other information that he in turn passed along to the crowd. If I were a fan, that would be the last vantage point I would select. Watching from rink level, a spectator is too often screened from a view of the puck, particularly with heavy traffic in front of the net. When I did radio broadcasts of hockey games, I liked to be situated as high as possible above the ice. That vantage point "slows down" the action.

Sitting between the two penalty boxes posed additional problems. Once when Philadelphia Flyers' "bad boy", Dave Schultz, was banished to the so-called "sin-bin", I gave a routine announcement which went something like this, "Philadelphia penalty, number 15, Dave Schultz, five minutes for fighting and two minutes for high sticking."

As per instructions, I repeated the announcement, whereupon Schultz, reaching toward me though the circular opening in the glass partition that separated him from me, "playfully" poked me with his stick. No wonder writers dubbed the Flyers the "Broad St. Bullies."

Hockey's rebirth in Denver is now an inspiring chapter in American sports lore. The new team, which transferred from Quebec City, is the Colorado Avalanche. Their march to the 1996 and 2001 Stanley Cup championships had their fanatical followers in a constant state of frenzy. McNichols arena fell to the wrecking ball and the team shares the new Pepsi Center with the Nuggets. The Broncos enjoy a new stadium as well. Coors Field is now the oldest major league venue in Denver and it opened in 1995! The level of fan support is unparalleled.

In 1979 I became a broadcaster on the Air Force Academy Football Network, airing the complete schedule of home and road games. My heavy concentration was on interviews with some commentary during the games. I worked two years with veteran play-by-play announcer, Cliff Dodge, then spent three seasons working alongside Gene Benson. Former Air Force Academy Coach, Ben Martin, served as analyst my last two years.

Broadcasting the 1982 All-American Bowl in Birmingham, Alabama was a special thrill. It was played at legendary Legion Field, scene of so many Alabama triumphs when Bear Bryant coached the Crimson Tide. Air Force outscored Vanderbilt in a shootout. Johnny Unitas was my halftime guest.

Bud Wilkinson, Paul Hornung, Terry Hanratty, George Connor, Moose Krause and Norm Van Brocklin all shared a microphone with me during Air Force broadcasts. Ken Hatfield was head coach for all five years of my involvement in Air Force Academy football. It would be impossible to meet a finer gentleman.

I did lengthy pre-game interviews with Hatfield. Ken was an Academic All-American on a National Championship Arkansas team that included Jimmy Johnson and Jerry Jones, who later combined to make history for the Dallas Cowboys.

Hatfield succeeded Bill Parcells in 1979 and brought the Falcons back to prominence. He was voted College Football Coach of the Year in 1983. His successor, Fisher DeBerry, achieved that honor as well.

I began a nightly sports interview program on KDEN, shunning subjects such as yesterday's victory or tomorrow's prospects. I concentrated on personal, human-interest angles, drawing out athletes to reveal their ambitions, their fears and uncertainties. How, for example, do they battle back, mentally and physically, from career threatening injuries? I asked them how they manage to stay calm and focused in moments of high intensity, what enables them to be at their best when stakes are highest.

Denver Broncos' players were frequent guests on my interview programs. Randy Gradishar talked emotionally about his love for one of college football's most severe taskmasters, Woody Hayes. Gradishar also expounded about the pain an inside linebacker had to endure in the dangerous and violent world of NFL football. I asked Gradishar to identify the part of his anatomy most abused by football. He didn't hesitate. "The hands, because of having to ward off 290 pound blockers in the opponents' offensive line."

Fans loved the relentless competitive spirit Gradishar unfailingly brought to every game. He was the prototype of a football warrior. Randy is a prominent member of the Broncos' "Ring of Fame."

Speaking of Denver Bronco football players, I asked Craig Morton to tell about how he and his Dallas Cowboys teammates coped with his borderline laryngitis in the days leading up to a Super Bowl. Coach Tom Landry assigned halfback Dan Reeves to chant signals while Morton rested his strained vocal cords.

My listeners would learn how John Elway coped with his first year of pro football pressure. During one interview, we ignored football to review Elway's brief but promising baseball career when he was a number one New York Yankees draft choice, playing right field and bashing the ball hard in the Pony League at Oneonta, New York.

The ebullient, Hank Stram, once joined me for an interview at Mile High Stadium. He was there to do a network telecast. Well-wishers by the dozen were greeting him. Hank could see we would need some privacy to do the interview. Like an officer leading his troops into battle, Hank said, "Follow me." He led us straight to the men's room and proceeded to lock the door. Even though it was the only press box comfort station, we did TWO separate interviews. I don't recall anyone rapping on the door.

University of Washington football coach, Rick Neuheisel, told me a bizarre story surrounding one of his greatest performances. It was the day he threw four touchdown passes and accumulated 298 passing yards in leading the UCLA Bruins to a lopsided victory over Illinois in the Rose Bowl. Neuheisel was awarded the Most Valuable Player honors for his effort.

CHAPTER 21: FROM "THE BULLIES"...

When I asked him how he felt taking the field before more than 103,000 fans that afternoon, he said he felt a great adrenaline rush. That morning he and a few teammates were miserably sick with food poisoning. Team doctors provided the stricken players with medicine. Fearful of side effects, Neuheisel decided against medicinal help. The pills made his teammates so woozy they dozed off in the UCLA locker room; spending the entire game asleep. The feeling of excitement was so great that Neuheisel pushed aside his nausea and went on to play the greatest football game of his life.

Neuheisel was a classic example of an athlete's Cinderella story. As a walk on, his first assignment was to hold the ball for place kicker, John Lee. He was fifth on the quarterback depth chart. I asked Rick why he chose to go to UCLA as a walk on. He replied he wanted to play college football at the top level and he was not highly recruited.

The story hardly ends there. He beat out Steve Bono as the starting quarterback at UCLA, then had a stint with the San Diego Gun Slingers of the United States Football League and gained further experience with the San Diego Chargers and Tampa Bay Buccaneers.

Neuheisel's story as a coach paralleled his UCLA playing career in that he first joined the UCLA staff as a volunteer assistant. By age 33, he was the second youngest Division One head coach in collegiate football when he ascended to that position in 1995 at the University of Colorado. He brought so many winning credentials to the table as the successor to Bill McCartney that age hardly seemed a factor. After all, Lou Boudreau was only 24 when he became playing manager of the Cleveland Indians in 1942.

Magic Johnson, sometimes in the manner of a trainer, would vividly describe the physical and mental torment of serious injury, followed by tortuous rehabilitation, and the accompanying nagging uncertainty of whether he would ever regain top form.

Doctor J. (Julius Erving) would describe in eloquent detail the ordeal of enduring excruciating pain in both of his knees. He would rise above the pain to reach his sport's pinnacle as the key player on the Philadelphia 76ers' NBA champions. Erving was always a gentleman and always considerate. Before I did a post game interview with him, he requested my permission to first take a hot shower to relieve the throbbing pain in his knees.

Erving then told me, "You're good for the sport of basketball and for the fans of Denver." When Philly at long last won the NBA crown in 1983, a writer described Erving "swooping and soaring like an avenging angel."

My listeners would hear James Worthy describe how blessed he was to have a special talent bestowed on him by his Maker, a talent he felt compelled to use and develop to the utmost. They would also hear a soft spoken and humble David Thompson casually discuss his phenomenal jumping and shooting ability. They would be recipients of the comments of outrageously outspoken, arrogant, and abrasive Red Auerbach, who led the Boston Celtics to an unprecedented and almost certainly never to be approached string of NBA championships.

I talked with refreshingly brash Danny Schayes, long an NBA journeyman. Schayes once tried to goad me into disposing of a stopwatch that had obviously seen better days. I told him, "Nothing doin'. That's a valuable antique."

I had inadvertently left a door open, for he replied, "But aren't you something of an antique yourself?"

So many personalities with so many fascinating stories to relate. An interviewer, once he gets his guest's confidence, can bring out innermost thoughts that are so revealing. Listeners appreciate gaining insight, not only into the success stories, but also into how athletes cope with hard times, slumps, injuries, failures and disappointments encountered in their fiercely competitive world.

22 DIMAGGIO, MANTLE AND THE SHOT

I have been fortunate to see and appreciate many uniquely gifted athletes. On the baseball diamond alone I watched legendary men including Babe Ruth, Lou Gehrig, Jimmy Foxx, Bob Feller, Ted Williams, Mickey Mantle, Willie Mays, Jackie Robinson, Stan Musial, Johnny Bench, Bob Gibson, Mark McGwire, and Sammy Sosa. But for sheer all-around talent, the greatest of them all was Joe DiMaggio, who towered above the rest.

The first time I saw DiMaggio was at Comiskey Park in 1936, Joe's rookie year. He was twenty-one. The home of the White Sox, with its vast outfield was definitely not hitter-friendly. It was kind of like old Yankee Stadium, so huge that it was where triples went to die. That day, DiMaggio did something I never again saw a major leaguer duplicate. He hit two home runs in the SAME INNING, including a monster wallop that crashed into the upper deck.

The Yankee Clipper's 56-game hitting streak in 1941 is the most astounding testament to consistency baseball has ever known. Another statistic without parallel is that DiMaggio slammed 361 homers, yet struck out only 369 times, an amazing ratio. Here is the true testament of Joe DiMaggio's worth. In the seven years before he joined them, the Yankees had won just one pennant. They became world champs in Joe D's first four seasons while compiling an eye-popping 16-3 World Series record. During Joe's 13 years with New York, the Yankees rolled to ten pennants and nine world championships.

The intensely private Joe DiMaggio was at various times referred to as stoic, aloof, standoffish, cold, morose, uncommunicative, and suspicious; but never rude. When I taped an interview with him, he was certainly not a jovial, backslapping guest. However, he accorded me total respect by listening to my questions and comments with undivided attention, and then enthusiastically participating in the interview.

He recalled the incredibly long hitting streak that captured the imagination of a sporting nation for two suspense-filled months. When I asked him what he remembered most about that record-shattering streak, he replied, "I'd say it was the day I was stopped. Ken Keltner of the Cleveland ball club made those two fantastic stops, then just nipped me at first base. It was just by a whisker, that he got me. It was a wonderful time that I had, Joe. I do recall that there was no guarantee at any time you'd play the whole game. Once I got my hit in the fourth inning. Then it rained during the fifth and suddenly it was an official game. I could easily have been wiped out then. Of course, there were a lot of games when I got my hit in the ninth inning."

I questioned Joe about blasting those two home runs in the same inning in his rookie year. His eyes lit up and he leaned forward slightly. "I remember, Joe! I hit those homers off old San Francisco pitcher, Italo Chelini." I was startled because of the rarity of DiMaggio's hitting two homers off the same pitcher, and said so.

He nodded. "They were hit my first two times at bat. They didn't take the pitcher out so fast in those days. It was the first inning and the White Sox were very much in the game."

Finally, I asked this baseball hero how much he missed the sport competitively the first year after his retirement. I watched as he rearranged his elegantly clad legs.

"My injuries caused me to retire early and that's why I didn't miss the game so much. Had I stayed healthy, I would have kept on playing and then gone out in a more usual way."

It was said he was a mass of bruises after every game from flinging himself at the bases. He endured ulcers, bone spurs, knee problems, and pneumonia. The pain while playing during those years was not so well known as it is now. He claimed he played hard in every game just in case someone was in the stands who had never seen him play before.

I thanked Joe for joining me for the interview. He leaned toward me with a warm handshake, saying, graciously, "Thank you, Joe, thank you so much."

Like no other in baseball's long history, Joe D. brought an unforgettable quality combining talent, grace, and majesty to the baseball diamond. As one writer so aptly put it, "Joe DiMaggio transcended the sport to become an American icon."

As for me, I shall always treasure those fond memories of Joltin" Joe DiMaggio, and what a quintessential gentleman he was for the brief time he shared with me.

The day I interviewed DiMaggio, I also interviewed Don Larsen and Bobby Thomson. These three wrote some of the most memorable episodes in the annals of baseball. DiMaggio's long hitting streak had to rank at the top as baseball's greatest single season achievement. No player ever had a day to match Don Larsen's perfect World Series game against the hard hitting Brooklyn Dodgers. Most assuredly, baseball never had a moment as exciting as Bobby Thomson's home run off Ralph Branca that gave the New York Giants a come-from-behind playoff victory over Brooklyn, and with it, the 1951 National League pennant.

Larsen told me he was fearful Casey Stengel wouldn't pitch him again because Don had faltered in a previous Series start. He recalled that his concentration was intensified because his pitching rival, Sal Maglie, was also holding the Yankees at bay. Larsen remembered how his knees shook as he took the mound for the suspenseful ninth inning.

Thomson reminisced about the long wait before stepping in against the gangling Ralph Branca. Brooklyn carried a 4-1 lead into the bottom of the ninth inning at the historic old Polo Grounds in north Manhattan. Alvin Dark led off and reached base against the overpowering Don Newcombe, who had given no evidence he would falter.

For some inexplicable reason, the Dodgers elected to hold Dark close to the bag, even with a three-run advantage. Don Mueller, who could handle a bat with anyone, took advantage of the Brooklyn defensive alignment and punched a sharp bouncing single through the yawning hole on the right side. Had Hodges been playing off the bag, as the game situation surely dictated, he could have made a play on Mueller's hard-hit ground ball, perhaps for a force out at second or even a double play. At worst, he could have retired Don at first. As it was, Dark scampered around to third as Carl Furillo fired back in.

Monte Irvin, who had the unenviable distinction of making the only out of baseball's most historic half inning, lifted a pop foul gathered in by Hodges. Responding to the challenge, Whitey Lockman refused to be suckered into pulling an outside pitch. He lashed a solid "gapper" into left center field as Dark scored and Mueller hot-footed it around to third.

Mueller sustained a broken ankle for his efforts and had to leave the game. Now it was 4-2 with two runners in scoring position, only one out. There was a lengthy delay while Mueller was being attended to, then carefully removed from the field on a stretcher. Lockman later declared he was "floatin'" after contributing his two-bagger.

During the extended break in action, Dressen signaled to the faraway bullpen and Branca started his long walk to the mound. The adjoining Polo Grounds bullpens were some 440 feet from the pitcher's mound.

Thomson told me he began to talk to himself as the din mounted. He kept saying, "Sit and wait, sit and wait." It was a pointed reminder to stay back and not lunge at the ball, to make Branca come to him.

Duke Snider remembers Branca's long walk in and telling Ralph as the big right hander passed him en route to the mound, "Go get 'im, Honk. You can do it."

Branca, normally a starter, was brought in because bullpen coach, Clyde Sukeforth, had informed Dressen on the connecting bullpen and dugout phone that Carl Erskine didn't have good stuff and that Clem Labine, also heating up, was "bouncing his curve ball."

Snider told me on an interview that he experienced a mild sense of alarm when Branca, at long last, arrived at the circle of the mound. Dressen would normally go face-to-face with his reliever, then give him an encouraging pat on the backside before returning to the dugout. But this time Charlie stood apart from Branca and merely flipped him the ball.

Thomson was still exhorting himself to be patient, to "sit and wait" as the ear-splitting uproar continued. Wait he did as Branca came in with a perfect strike. Bobby's intent was to make hard contact. Most likely a single would produce two runs and elevate the Giants into a 4-4 deadlock. Branca swung into his windup, fired and Thomson snapped his wrists. Contact was made and the world stood still. The distance to the left field fence at the foul pole in the horseshoe-shaped Polo Grounds was a mere 279 feet. If a hitter pulled the ball close to the foul line, he could often reach the seats with a routine fly ball. Thomson hit a semi-line drive that never did gain much altitude.

Dodger center fielder, Duke Snider, vividly remembers left fielder, Andy Pafko, drifting back, hoping to make a play on the ball or at least field it quickly off the short barrier. Duke then saw Pafko had no further room to maneuver as Thomson's drive reached the seats. Bobby remembers running hard, hoping the ball would at least hit the wall so two runs could score and he would be able to reach second base.

The overwhelming crowd noise, coupled with the umpire's signal, informed him that he had indeed hit a pennant-winning home run thus becoming an immortal figure in baseball history.

Snider remembers that the champagne that had been put on ice in the Dodgers' clubhouse was now being transported to the Giants' locker room as frenzy combined with heartbreak on that unforgettable October afternoon. Snider remembers Branca sobbing in the clubhouse, inconsolably moaning, "Why me?"

Eventually I interviewed several players who were part of the ninth inning drama that day, including Thomson, Lockman, Dark, Irvin, Snider, Newcombe, Reese, and Dodgers' manager, Dressen. Each had his own special recollections of the heart-stopping inning.

Despite its vast population, the New York City area didn't contribute a very large percentage of players that reached the majors. Yet the principal figures in the pitcher/batter drama that fateful afternoon were Branca, from Mount Vernon, N.Y. and Thomson, a native of Glasgow, Scotland but later a resident of Staten Island, N.Y. In fact, he became known as the "Slammin' Scot from Staten Island."

Mickey Mantle joined me one day on the radio and recounted his biggest World Series home run. It was a sudden death blast off the upper deck facade at Yankee Stadium in 1964. That homer broke Babe Ruth's World Series home run record. Mantle recalled he told on-deck hitter, Elston Howard, his plan of attack. Knuckleballer, Barney Schultz, had just been waved in from the St. Louis Cardinals' bullpen. Mantle correctly surmised Schultz would strive extra hard to throw a strike on the first pitch and, because of this, Barney would sacrifice some deception and movement of the ball. Sure enough, Mickey had guessed right and whaled away. Moments later, a dejected Schultz descended from the mound in tears, a World Series loser despite throwing only one pitch!

Another time I interviewed Mantle in Fort Lauderdale, where he was a Yankees' spring training coach. I asked Mickey what he missed least about the game after his retirement as a player, suggesting perhaps the frequent travelling or living in hotels, constantly packing or unpacking. I should have refrained from any hint of putting words into his mouth; never a good idea.

He startled me by saying, "What I miss least of all are the interviews with writers and broadcasters." I was slightly taken aback but couldn't question his forthright reply.

Mantle may have been the greatest pure athlete ever to play baseball. What is the definition of a near perfect athlete? He'd have speed, quickness, sharp timing, razor like reflexes, marvelously developed hand-eye coordination, explosiveness, aggressiveness, courage, and a burning competitive desire. Mantle in his heyday possessed all of these attributes in abundance. No player in baseball history ever had his combination of raw speed and colossal power from BOTH sides. Just try to name one other home run slugger who could bunt for a base hit like Mantle could do when the bunt was in order. Had Mickey taken care of himself properly and had he been fortunate to have escaped injuries, he might have firmly established himself as the greatest ever.

Who was baseball's greatest ambassador during and after his playing career? I'm sure there would be many worthy choices. Based on first hand experience, I would give the nod to Bob Feller. I've spent countless hours with Feller, accompanying him to appearances at ballparks, restaurants, car dealerships and industries in both Rochester and Denver. I was once with him for 12 hours in Rochester. He arrived by plane in the early morning from Cleveland and was whisked through a day so full he barely had time for lunch. Never once did he complain. The only time he requested a break was to make a telephone call back to his insurance business in Cleveland. He even appeared on my broadcast from the ballpark that night, 14 hours after his arrival.

I've seen Feller sign hundreds of free autographs in the same day. No athlete could have been more generous with his time. Once when Bob came to Denver to appear at Mile High Stadium and pitch to media members (he did that annually) he discovered the Bears were about to play a day-night double header. He had contracted to perform at night but offered his services FREE for the afternoon game, too. I turned him down, but I've never forgotten that selfless gesture. Feller had no false humility. He was and is fully aware of his stature as an all-time great, but he didn't tiresomely flaunt his achievements.

Feller was impressed when my wife, Ottie, accompanied me to meet him at the Rochester airport. I'll never forget his response.

"It's not as if I were Cary Grant," he remarked.

Rapid Robert obviously developed a strong work ethic while growing up on a farm outside Van Meter, Iowa. To this day he has never abandoned those industrious habits. Feller, as you might suspect, is an outstanding interview guest. He had occasion to polish his microphone skills when he was one of Mutual's "Game of the Day" broadcasters in the fifties and sixties. One of Feller's deepest regrets was never winning a World Series game.

Feller remembered being victimized by one of the worst non-calls in Series history. Rapid Robert was locked up in a scoreless pitcher's duel with Boston's Johnny Sain in the ninth inning of game one in the 1948 Series. Phil Masi was the runner at second base with one out. Shortstop and manager, Lou Boudreau, broke to cover second base; Feller whirled and threw to the bag. Masi was caught dead to rights. Boudreau had the ball waiting for the trapped runner as he slid in but second base umpire, Bill Stewart, wasn't watching. He was looking up into the stands and admitted as much afterward. The batter, Tommy Holmes, then stroked a soft single into left field and Masi scampered home with the game's only run.

Feller had one last chance to record a World Series victory when he took the hill before 85,000 onlookers at vast Cleveland Municipal Stadium four days later and was driven from the mound.

The night before the Cleveland Indians met the Boston Red Sox in a one-game showdown for that 1948 American League pennant, Indians' outfielder, Bob Kennedy, told second baseman, Joe Gordon, he was too keyed up to fall asleep as the train carried the Cleveland ball club to Boston.

Gordon said, "No problem, just take one of these," whereupon both ball players swallowed a strong sleeping potion. When they awakened the following morning, they discovered their teammates had already left the train, headed for Fenway Park. Kennedy told me he and Gordon were both frantic. Both were scheduled to be in the starting lineup, Kennedy in right field and Gordon at his customary infield position.

The two veterans spotted a nearby cafe and hurriedly wolfed down scrambled eggs and milk shakes before hailing a taxi to the ballpark for the biggest game of their baseball lives. They arrived with little time to spare and participated in the historic battle during which manager, Lou Boudreau, rapped out four hits, including two homers in leading Cleveland to an 8-3 conquest. That was the game in which Boudreau gave his charges the option of naming the starting pitcher, whereupon the players threw that weighty decision right back on their skipper. Boudreau nominated Gene Bearden, a left-hander.

Southpaws don't typically fare well in Fenway Park because of the uncomfortably close "Green Monster" in left field. But Bearden was outstanding as he pitched the Tribe into the World Series.

23 MONTANA, REEVES, MADDEN & A FEW OTHER FOOTBALL NOTABLES

Hardest place to conduct an interview? I found it to be the visitors' football locker room at Mile High Stadium, following a tough-to-swallow defeat. Players are often in a surly, angry mood in those circumstances. The importance of each contest is magnified by the limited schedule of 16 games in contrast to basketball's 82 or baseball's 162 game schedule. The old cliche and battle cry "We'll get 'em next time" just doesn't apply in football.

My policy when interviewing players following a game has always been to wait as long as possible. Give them a chance to cool down. Let the emotional intensity and the physical ordeal of violent, bone-jarring battle gradually subside.

Some players are reluctant to talk after a difficult defeat. When that occurs, I don't press them. But most, when approached properly and not in a pushy manner, will consent to be interviewed. I remember becoming very angry after doing an aborted interview with Joe Montana during a San Francisco 49ers visit to Mile High Stadium.

Joe was easy to meet; by no means an exciting guest but interesting, attentive and informative. We had reached midpoint of a four-minute interview, whereupon I made the routine pause for a commercial break.

"We'll be back with Joe Montana after this message."

Then I said, "Three, two, one," so the engineer later could cue tape to the remainder of the interview.

While I was giving the "cutaway cue," an overbearing 49ers publicity man, without bothering to inquire whether I had concluded my conversation, abruptly whisked Joe away, saying "C'mon, it's time to board the team bus."

I could have punched the lout, but had no time to spare. I revised my cutaway cue on the tape to, "We'll be back with more football after this message." Then I devoted the remaining time to Keith Fahnhorst, an offensive tackle who was still getting dressed. What, I wondered, was the hurry with Montana and the publicity man? Fahnhorst affably agreed to be interviewed. To tie it in with my discussion with Montana, I had Keith expound on the techniques of pass blocking for his illustrious teammate.

The Denver Broncos were a joy to work with. I interviewed Dan Reeves covering a wide range of subjects, including the state of his health following treatment for heart problems. He talked about what he was doing to correct unhealthy eating habits and how he would struggle to control his quick-triggered temper on the sidelines in the heat of battle. Equally important, he pointed out how he would find time to relax during the hectic season. Dan couldn't have been more accommodating to me.

CHAPTER 23: MONTANA, REEVES, MADDEN...

I remember experiencing the warm feeling when Broncos' Public Relations Director, Jim Saccomano, told me Randy Gradishar had approached him and said what a pleasure it was to have a "real radio man" like me interview him.

Saccomano is the epitome of what a media relations director should be. Whenever I required his assistance, either in setting up interviews or in supplying me with pertinent information about the Broncos or other NFL teams, Saccomano was ever available. This was important in John Elway's rookie year. Elway was hounded by local, regional, and national media. It was impossible to get near him without Saccomano's help. I didn't have unlimited time at my disposal because I worked full time for the Denver Bears. I did these football interviews principally during my lunch hour.

One time a Broncos' player spotted me on the practice field and said he'd enjoy being interviewed by me. I had interviewed him during previous seasons. The player was Tom Jackson. I was deeply touched by his special and rare kindness. How many athletes in any sport go that far in making themselves accessible to a media member? Jackson has risen high in his own broadcasting career, working comfortably with the likes of Chris Berman, Robin Roberts, Joe Theisman and Chris Mortenson on ESPN. Jackson truly is one of the nation's best studio analysts.

Gigantic nose tackle, Rubin Carter, was always a delight to interview, chuckling good-naturedly whenever I would needle him in a friendly manner. Two of the Broncos I came to know better than I knew their teammates were kicking specialists, punter Luke Prestridge and bare-footed place kicker, Rich Karlis. Since they were not required to attend most noon time players' meetings, I spent many enjoyable times kibitzing with them at the Broncos' practice facility. Prestridge was a baseball addict who had played both sports for Baylor University and might well have pursued a baseball career had not football intervened.

The Oakland (later Los Angeles and then again, the Oakland) Raiders' locker room was always an interesting and, at times, a challenging place to visit. I once came across Al Davis, nattily attired in all white, reminding me of the "Good Humor" ice cream man who would hawk his wares in the neighborhood of my boyhood in Chicago. Fully aware that I might be rudely rebuffed, I was about to approach this controversial and fascinating man, but my recorder was malfunctioning when I tested it. The chance never came again.

Lester Hayes, the Raiders' storied cornerback, had a speech problem that caused him to stutter almost incessantly. I had recently read that Hayes had taken speech lessons trying to overcome his impediment and that his stuttering had appreciably diminished. Arms, wrists, hands and elbows covered with his trademark "Stickum", Lester happily agreed to be interviewed. We proceeded, but he still stuttered so noticeably that it would have been an injustice to him to play the tape over the air. I discarded it regretfully because Lester was an intelligent and most entertaining personality.

Shortly after he abandoned coaching and became a fabulously successful broadcaster, I interviewed John Madden. He elaborated on his fear of flying, that he felt agonizingly trapped when airborne. He revealed how happy he was to have abandoned that mode of travel. He discussed the disappearance of his ulcers after being separated from the rigors of coaching for Al Davis, but was never critical of Al.

When I commented he sounded so much the natural, even in his earliest television days, he replied that he didn't find it all that easy, that it was important to "...be yourself but with clearly defined parameters." I remember Madden declaring he hardly missed coaching, only the "competition of Sunday."

When I interviewed Pat Summerall, he recalled being frightened when doing a radio sports show for the first time in New York when he was still place kicking for the Giants. He had been interviewed many times as a player, but he quickly discovered how different and difficult it could be when he was cast in the role of initiating the conversation. There was no flamboyance in the Pat Summerall I met, just the same restrained personality who has gained the respect of sports fans all across America. That applies whether he's describing football, golf, or tennis. He's obviously an expert, always understating rather than hyping his subject. Curiously, this trait of understating somehow adds to Summerall's dramatic appeal. Have you heard more contrasting styles than the Madden/Summerall duo? It's an important part of what makes them an ideal team.

Howard Cosell was so preposterous I found him entertaining. I still miss him, particularly on Monday Night Football, where he had countless detractors. Howard was never in awe of anyone. However, he had an irritating tendency to dominate his guests, many of whom were not comfortable with him.

Bob Costas conducts an outstanding interview. He's ALWAYS prepared. It's easy to see why Bob has been the recipient of many national awards, all richly deserved, including Sportscaster of the Year commendations. I've never met Costas and perhaps I'm guilty of nit-picking, but he comes across as perhaps a bit too cocksure of his ability. There is a hint of smugness that pervades his work, whether he's a studio host or interviewer. This never stops me from listening to what he has to say. His expertise is undeniable and he's an accomplished play-by-play man, too. I've often followed Costas through entire programs, including lengthy ones, during which he didn't make a single mistake. That quality of concentration is admirable.

The symbol of the ESPN's success is Chris Berman, who has been on the scene almost from the start. Berman has received many awards for sportscasting excellence. There is no denying his vast knowledge of NFL football, and his fine grasp of the sport's intricacies. He's extremely popular with a multitude of viewers and works well with studio cohorts, Tom Jackson, Robin Roberts, Joe Theisman and Chris Mortenson. Perhaps I should join the legions of Berman's boosters, but I don't enjoy him. He's much too bombastic to suit my tastes, and he comes across as being something of an exhibitionist. I've reached the point that when his "fastest two minutes of football" comes on during Sunday evening NFL wrap-ups, I'm sorely tempted to turn the sound down, or completely off.

Among broadcasters whose specialties are in-depth feature interviews, my favorite is Roy Firestone. He is a master at drawing out guests, no matter how touchy or controversial

CHAPTER 23: MONTANA, REEVES, MADDEN... 225

the subject matter. Never reluctant to pose tough questions, he has the ability to playfully needle his guests without alienating them. It's obvious he comes to his program fully prepared. There always seems to be a camaraderie between Roy and his guests, who seem to appreciate his sensitivity and respect for them.

Colorado Rockies baseball fans were fortunate to have a television analyst who could have made it big even if he had never played professionally. Dave Campbell, now with ESPN, played big league baseball, principally in the role of utility infielder. He also managed in the higher minors. Dave brings so much more than pure expertise to his telecasts. He has an excellent facility with words and good voice animation, fully capable of conveying excitement when the situation demands it. Campbell has a wealth of interesting stories, a bright sense of humor and a knack of conveying baseball nuances without boring or overwhelming his listeners. Campbell can step nimbly from the analyst role into play-by-play as smoothly as anyone I've ever heard. He works effectively with compatriots and NEVER interrupts when his partner is describing action.

Former major league pitcher, George Frazier, now excels as the Rockies' analyst.

Another ex-player who fits the requirements of a professional announcer is former National Football League star, Dave Logan. He has a pleasant voice with a command of the language and sharp sense of humor. Whether handling color in football or basketball, he has an uncanny ability to dissect strategy without being ponderous or dull. He both entertains and informs with an almost perfect balance. His versatility is most impressive. Logan is one of the few former ex-athletes I've heard who can step from the booth into a studio and anchor a daily four-hour talk show. He converses easily and exchanges barbs with his co-host, Scott Hastings, another former athlete. Dave handles callers' questions with intelligence and patience. He responds with insightful answers. Logan never seems to lose his aplomb while switching back and forth between television and radio.

Denver's best young sports announcer, in my opinion, is Drew Goodman, a Brooklyn native and product of Ithaca College. His football and basketball play-by-play is crisp and easy to follow. He conveys excitement without over-dramatizing. Drew is adept at doing interviews.

Goodman became the Colorado Rockies' television play-by-play broadcaster beginning in 2002. He also is the Denver Nuggets announcer. As a studio talk show host, he exhibits patience with callers and is never rude, even to those with whom he disagrees sharply. Goodman's versatility is impressive in both radio and television. He slips easily from one medium to the other.

24 STAY ALERT AND BE READY TO DUCK

There are enough injuries in the normal course of sports competition that freak mishaps can drive coaches and managers batty. Consider two that happened when I announced Rochester games. Pitcher Jim Hardin stepped on a stingray in shallow Atlantic Ocean waters at Daytona Beach during spring training and was incapacitated for six weeks. Our old friend, Frank "Toys in the Attic" Bertaina, called up to Baltimore for the express purpose of starting game three of the 1966 World Series, tripped on a ball bag while running outfield sprints, sustained a sprained ankle and thereby lost his big chance.

A much more serious accident could have occurred during a Governor's Cup playoff game I described in Rochester. Syracuse relief pitchers, Bill Faul and Tom Timmerman, traded punches in the Chiefs' bullpen. Faul, a flaky sort, was tossing lighted firecrackers around and Timmerman took issue. Timmerman got the better of the brawl with his eccentric teammate. When I visited the Syracuse clubhouse the next night in an attempt to learn more of the particulars, a firecracker came dangerously close to me. I was sufficiently frightened to beat a hasty retreat. That clubhouse was hardly a safe haven.

I've always had a keen admiration for athletes who possess courage and determination to overcome major physical obstacles. I think of successful Detroit Tigers' pitchers of widely separated eras, Hal Newhouser and John Hiller, dominating American League batters despite persistent heart problems. Then there were diabetics like Ron Santo and tennis standouts of the fifties and sixties, Hamilton Richardson and Billy Talbert who carved out brilliant careers.

Others triumphed over physical problems. Jim Abbott achieved pitching success despite the absence of a hand from birth. Pete Gray played in the wartime St. Louis Browns' outfield in 1944 even though he had only one arm. Red Schoendienst overcame a long and difficult bout with tuberculosis during his playing career. That, however, didn't prevent him from achieving Hall of Fame status. Schoendienst finally submitted to a successful operation that enabled him to conquer his affliction. He told me during the 1994 season that he felt better at 71 than he did at 21!

When I announced Texas League games in Houston, the ball club had a Cuban curve baller named Octavio Rubert, blind in one eye. One time Rubert was struck on the leg by a vicious line drive. As anxious teammates gathered around him at the mound, he fixed his stare on each of them and declared, none too assuredly, "I peetch, but you be ready."

I once saw Brooklyn first baseman, Buddy Hassett, suffer a fractured skull when beaned by a fast ball delivered by the Cubs' Roy Parmalee. From high up in the stands you could hear the sickening sound of the baseball crashing against his head. Those were pre-helmet days. Yet Buddy came back to play several more years of solid big league baseball.

I sadly watched two careers come to a premature end because of frightening bean balls. In 1954, while describing a Houston Buffs' game, I watched power hitting outfielder Sonny Senerchia, who earlier had played with the Pittsburgh Pirates' "Kiddie Corps", take a fast ball flush to his skull. He didn't have the benefit of a batting helmet. For days he struggled to remain alive. Coached gently by Dixie Walker, Senerchia attempted valiantly to come back but couldn't avoid an inadvertent flinch, which became a reflex action on any inside pitch. He couldn't rise above his fear of being hit again. Reluctantly, Senerchia abandoned his once-promising career.

Rochester's 1969 ball club had an infielder, Chico Fernandez, who had played with Baltimore the previous year. Chico was still plagued with a sore arm, so he was basically a bench-warmer, relegated to an occasional pinch-hitting or pinch-running assignment. One evening as darkness approached during a twi-night double header, manager, Cal Ripken, called on Fernandez to pinch-hit. It was a difficult time to see the ball, not dark enough for the lights to have fully taken hold.

Chico's reflexes were understandably rusty from inactivity. Furthermore, when summoned by Ripken, he couldn't locate his batting helmet with an earflap. He donned a helmet without one. That proved to be a near fatal error in judgment. Tidewater Tides pitcher, Larry Bearnarth, came high and tight with a fast ball, a purpose pitch with no design other than to prevent Chico from digging in. Fernandez lost sight of the pitch tailing in. The next instant he was writhing on the ground. He reached for his left ear, which regrettably could have been protected by the earflap. Chico never lost consciousness. He was rushed to a nearby hospital and a brain surgeon commenced operating. For approximately 48 hours, Chico's life hung in the balance. Finally, the period of grave danger ended.

Even as he began his slow recovery, Fernandez was horrified by his inability to speak fluently from the resulting brain damage. Steel plates were inserted in his head. A native of Puerto Rico, Chico took speech lessons for over a year in a dogged and ultimately successful attempt to regain mastery of two languages, Spanish and English.

Fernandez attempted to come back as a Rochester coach in 1971 but wasn't ready and, sadly, was forced to resume rehabilitation. Several years later, I had firsthand proof of his full recovery. At a spring training exhibition game, we had a joyous reunion in Vero Beach, Florida. By that time, Chico was wearing the uniform of the Los Angeles Dodgers as a minor league hitting instructor.

Even in the days before batting helmets became mandatory, most pitchers weren't the least bit reluctant to come inside on hitters. That has always been an important part of a pitcher's arsenal—to strike the element of fear into a batter, just enough so the hitter wouldn't be too eager to "dive" into a pitch on the outside portion of home plate.

I remember a Texas League batter forced to hit the dirt to avoid a pitch coming toward his head, delivered by Houston fireballer, Jack Cardey. The batter glared at Cardey; then, bat still in hand, strode menacingly toward the mound. It looked like High Noon but no one intervened. Just before he reached the hill to confront his staring adversary, the player dropped his bat and tore into Cardey, who received a savage pummeling. No one left the dugout. Players and umpires just let the two combatants settle their own differences.

I saw one other beating administered in Houston. Due to early season rainouts in 1954, Houston and Ft. Worth were forced to play four consecutive double headers in the dog days of August. Ft. Worth's pitching standout was the phenomenal Karl Spooner, who later that year struck out 27 batters in his first two major league starts for the Brooklyn Dodgers. The Buffs and Cats were deadlocked for first place as the big series began.

Houston proceeded to blow the race apart by winning the first seven games! As the teams were playing an anticlimactic eighth contest, a fan who had been incessantly taunting Al Vincent, the Ft. Worth manager and first base coach, continued his loud, derisive comments. Vincent, known as "The Gray Fox" because of his silver mane, suddenly went berserk. He raced toward the box seats and leaped over the railing. His bewildered antagonist seemed unable to defend himself against Vincent's furious attack and absorbed a brutal beating that included multiple rabbit punches to the neck. Police and ushers didn't respond immediately and the beleaguered fan was at the mercy of the wild-eyed assailant.

The fan, fortunate to escape with his life, sued Vincent. Texas League President, John Reeves, got into the act by publicly proclaiming that Houston officials didn't protect fans with adequate policing. Houston General Manager, Art Routzong, angrily took issue with Reeves. I don't know whether one could point to cause and effect, but Reeves soon was ousted as Texas League President and replaced by Dick Butler.

Does a broadcaster venturing onto the playing field ever get hit with a baseball? I've been hit several times, once a hard shot flush on the kneecap. Another time, during batting practice, I was walking toward the clubhouse deep down the right field line at Mile High Stadium, when I was hit on the top of the head with a hard hit ball. I bled from the blow but was indeed fortunate. Had I turned my head I could have been hit in the face or eye. There is no safe place on the field. You take your chances.

The broadcast booth can be a dangerous place, depending on the announcer's proximity to the field. In Des Moines the announcer's vantage point is so close to the diamond that foul balls whiz in so rapidly the baseball is hardly more than a blur. There's often almost no time to duck.

When Mickey Mantle joined me in the booth in Rochester, even though our lofty perch afforded considerably more reaction time than was available in Des Moines, Mickey quickly backed off when a foul ball approached. I chided him for ducking, whereupon the sheepish former superstar admitted, "The closer the ball came, the more it picked up speed." Right on, Mickey.

My daughter, Susie, has a painful memory of baseball in Rochester. Sitting in the radio booth with me, she was struck on the mouth by a rapidly travelling foul ball that appeared to be accelerating as it came in. She was helped from the booth, bleeding and crying, but fortunately with teeth intact. Never again did she watch a game from the booth.

25 RENEWING AN ACQUAINTANCE WITH DON BAYLOR

When major league baseball arrived in Denver, I waited awhile before contacting Don Baylor, who surely would be overwhelmed by the challenge of meeting so many people. When I called Don in his clubhouse office, it was the first time I had talked with him in more than 21 years, dating back to 1972 spring training in Miami when he was an Orioles' rookie. Baylor had no way of knowing I was living in Denver. He immediately invited me to visit him. Don warmly greeted me in his clubhouse office, about six hours prior to game time. We had a grand time reminiscing and bringing each other up to date.

The get-together occurred while Baylor's team was bogged down in a thirteen-game tailspin. Before the game had started, home plate umpire, Charlie Williams, ejected Baylor. It was the continuation of a sharp disagreement between the two from the previous night.

At the time I had no media connection, but Don insisted I visit him whenever it suited me and to make myself at home on the field and in the clubhouse. Don personally called the Rockies' publicity office to have credentials delivered to me. That was indeed a kind gesture. I didn't wish to abuse Baylor's hospitality so I limited the number of times I accepted his offer.

Baylor was unique among major league baseball expansion managers. He established a record by taking the Rockies into the post-season playoffs in only their third year of existence. That achievement was duly acknowledged when Don was named National League Manager of the Year in 1995.

Early in the 1994 season, John McHale, Jr., Rockies Vice President for Baseball Operations offered me the opportunity to do dozens of recorded interviews with Rockies and other National League players and managers. McHale commented that my wealth of baseball knowledge needed to find an outlet. He further stated that Bob Gebhard, the General Manager, felt the same way. Gebhard and I had formed a close friendship at the time I announced Denver Bears' games when the team was affiliated with Montreal. McHale paid me handsomely for each interview and planned to find a radio outlet to carry them.

From my first interview with enigmatic New York Mets' pitcher Bret Saberhagen (he was later traded to the Rockies) to the last with effervescent Dante Bichette on the final day before the players' sad walkout on August 11, I found it a joy to do the interviews. I felt as though I had never been away.

Several National League luminaries participated wholeheartedly, including low key Jeff Bagwell and his bubbling Houston teammate, Craig Biggio. The Giants' big bopper, introspective Matt Williams, was willing to relive the painful experience of his team's losing the Western Division championship on the final day of the 1993 season.

Manager, Dusty Baker, admitted he was so sad and wrought up over the Giants losing the West that for weeks afterward he made mindless daily trips to the ballpark. Finally, his wife and daughter convinced him of the sheer folly of trying to alter the past, even if only in his imagination.

I cornered the jovial Tom LaSorda, shooting bolts of electricity right through the microphone. Cubs' catcher Rick Wilkins, one of the game's most proficient at thwarting would-be base stealers, expounded on how he developed the footwork so necessary to his quick release. He was once a wrestler and needed deft footwork in order to capture an early edge as he and his opponent went to the mat.

Don Baylor took my listeners into the dugout during the most exciting inning of his illustrious playing career when he walloped a pinch-hit home run to help the Boston Red Sox win the American League championship over the California Angels. That was the LCS when Gene Mauch's ball club was one out removed from the World Series and never got there.

Ozzie Smith told me he was at first reluctant to join the St. Louis Cardinals in a trade from San Diego. Redbirds' Manager Whitey Herzog assured Ozzie that his arrival would immediately make St. Louis a title contender. That's exactly what transpired as Ozzie's three World Series appearances attest. Smith revealed that performing at top level at the demanding shortstop position, despite his advancing years, required punishing conditioning drills during the off season. The older he got, the harder he worked.

Former San Francisco Giants' coach, Bobby Bonds, went into great detail in describing how Willie Mays helped him develop into a first rate defensive outfielder. Bonds modestly reviewed his consistent success in two offensive categories that are rarely found in one player, hitting thirty or more home runs and stealing a like number of bases.

Joe Torre divulged why he left the comparative comfort and security of the broadcast booth to take on managing the St. Louis Cardinals. He hungered for competition and could handle the relentless pressure. In fact, he thrives on it. Torre moved to the Yankees and is piling up World Series rings.

Former Colorado Rockies' trainer, Dave Ciladi, took my audience through the step-by-step process of Andres Galarraga's agonizingly slow, painful rehabilitation after injuries in 1991 and '92. Ciladi stressed how important it was for the "Big Cat" to work with him several hours a day to restore his body to full health. Ciladi explained that trainer and player had to unite as a team and focus relentlessly on making it back. Galarraga's 1993 statistics, including a batting title, led to recognition as National League Comeback Player of the Year. It was that same determination that helped Galarraga beat cancer a few years later.

It was a treat to interview the Dodgers' lyrical voice, Vin Scully. He has described so many games that are an integral part of baseball history. Scully recalled eating breakfast just hours before his first World Series broadcast and how he "threw it up" at the prospect of speaking to such a vast audience. Scully went into considerable detail about what a severe taskmaster Red Barber was. Scully, however, added, "I loved Red as I did my own father".

Jack Buck reminisced about Bob Gibson, the fiercest competitor he ever met. Buck also expounded on broadcasting the historic 1967 National Football League championship game. Dubbed the Ice Bowl, The Green Bay Packers prevailed over the Dallas Cowboys. Buck remembered it was 17 degrees below when he received his wake-up call that morning.

I interviewed former Denver sports writer, Frank Haraway, many times. Frank covered minor league baseball in Denver for four decades before his retirement. He'd have been a success had he chosen a broadcasting career. He is an articulate and a proficient ad-libber with a resonant voice. He was the Colorado Rockies' official scorer in the team's early years.

The Atlanta Braves', Skip Caray, excitedly recounted his most thrilling and gratifying moment as a sportscaster. It was his description of the dramatic last inning pinch hit single by Francisco Cabrera that won the 1992 National League pennant. Cabrera's hit came in the seventh game and sent the Braves to the World Series over a stunned Pirates team.

Atlanta manager Bobby Cox recalled his first major league game as a New York Yankees' third baseman under Ralph Houk. During the pre-game introductions at hallowed Yankee Stadium, Cox shivered, then developed a painful leg cramp. He also told of the overwhelming task of doubling as general manager and manager in Toronto before going to Atlanta. Cox described replacement surgery on both knees that finally freed him from pain that had become difficult to endure. Bobby led Atlanta to victory in the 1995 World Series.

Tom Glavine, a native of the Boston area, told me he received offers to play professional hockey, but turned them down to pursue a baseball career. He was a hockey center, a playmaking specialist who relied on finesse, just as he still does on the baseball mound.

I talked to Greg Maddux when he was en route to his fourth consecutive Cy Young Award. He detailed his own analysis of how he achieved the pinnacle despite possessing, by his own admission, "no more than ordinary big league stuff." He described his keen disappointment when he discovered the floundering Cubs no longer desired his services, even though his initial Cy Young recognition came when he toiled for Chicago.

Tony Gwynn of San Diego, an eight time batting champ, admitted his obsession with videotapes. Watching tape often enables him to spot the tiniest mechanical flaws that might bring about a slump. Emerging swiftly from those mild batting letdowns has been perhaps the biggest single factor in his consistent hitting success.

Orel Hershiser brought to mind the dark days that befell him following a rotator cuff injury and how strong faith helped him to survive and extend a brilliant career.

Tim McCarver had riveting comments about catching two of the greatest pitchers of their era, Bob Gibson and Steve Carlton. When I sought out McCarver during a New York Mets' visit to Denver, I asked a Mets' player if he knew whether telecaster McCarver had made the trip. Amazingly, the player didn't know. I looked about twenty feet to my left and there stood McCarver, always an intriguing guest and, in my opinion, as fine an analyst as there is in baseball.

CHAPTER 25: RENEWING AN ACQUAINTANCE...

Former Cubs' analyst, Steve Stone, smoothly teamed with Harry Caray. Stone's expertise isn't limited to pitching, even though he's a former Cy Young Award winner who once went 25-7 for Earl Weaver's Orioles. Stone is a keen observer of baseball's nuances and has a facility with words that rivals many who have been professional announcers for decades.

During the aborted 1994 season, I did 143 interviews at Denver's Mile High Stadium with 135 different baseball personalities, each with his own fascinating and unique story to relate.

One of my most enthusiastic guests was former Houston Manager, Larry Dierker, also formerly an analyst on Houston Astros' broadcasts. Larry was once a standout Houston pitcher, a 20-game winner, an All Star, and had pitched a no-hitter. Larry remembered he was in a typical anti-social mood on the day he pitched his masterpiece. Like most hurlers, Dierker preferred privacy on days he was scheduled to pitch, the better to retreat into his shell of concentration.

Larry recalled that the day he fired his no-hitter coincided with his wedding anniversary. He had already stashed away a bottle of champagne, anticipating the customary anniversary celebration. Little did he envision there would be double cause to celebrate. Surprisingly, he most remembered his mistakes while carving the no-hit gem. He departed from his pre-game battle plan, throwing too many fast balls at a time in his career when his velocity wasn't as intimidating as it once was.

Dierker mailed me sample tapes of a program he broadcast daily in Houston during the off-season. It was called

"The Baseball Library" and zeroes in on historic events, tying them in to specific dates. He invited me to submit some of my own material covering baseball history. I sent him an interview I did with Joe DiMaggio and another on Mickey Mantle's recollections of the game winning tape measure home run he blasted to shatter Babe Ruth's World Series career home run record.

Also in 1994, I journeyed to Grand Junction, Colorado, to broadcast all nineteen games played during the eight days of the annual Junior College World Series. I had never before broadcast FOUR baseball games in one day, but I eagerly welcomed the challenge. It reminded me of doing six basketball games in one day at the Illinois High School State Tournament. I went on the air with color announcer Derry Newby at 8:45 a.m. and didn't finish game four until 10:30 that night. There was no time to eat until a brief break at about 6:30 that evening when I crossed the street to wolf down an Arby's roast beef sandwich. To quench my thirst and to remain reasonably sharp, I gulped down several, what seemed like a hundred, caffeine-laden drinks.

I told New York Mets' announcer, Bob Murphy, (we were both Texas League broadcasters many years before) of broadcasting four games in a single day. He promptly questioned my sanity. Keeping track of more than 200 ball players I had never heard of before constituted a formidable challenge. But I enjoyed it. In addition to play-by-play, I did pre-game interviews and also went down onto the field after games to interview winning managers.

I was impressed by the huge throng at the pre-tournament banquet during which pitching greats Tom Seaver, and

Rollie Fingers, spoke. Rollie still sports the "Snidely Whiplash" handlebar mustache that was his trademark when he was "Rollickin' Rollie", the relief pitching hero of the Oakland A's World Series teams.

Sam Suplizio Field, long-time site of the Junior College World Series, compares favorably with many Triple A parks from which I announced games. It's an immaculately maintained diamond that features a crushed brick infield surface, similar to the one at Dodger Stadium. It's a lightning fast infield, but true hops are the rule. In earlier years, the JUCO World Series site shifted frequently, but it has been a Grand Junction fixture since 1959. The tournament has become synonymous with Grand Junction.

Many current major leaguers have played in JUCO, using it as a stepping stone to launch pro careers. Big league scouts galore can be seen at every game. Quite often players are signed before they ever leave Colorado's Western Slope. The leading graduate of the event is Kirby Puckett, the Minnesota Twins' Hall of Famer.

26 KNUCKLERS & KNUCKLEHEADS

Knuckleballers, like place kickers or punters, are special characters. Because throwing the pitch puts virtually no strain on a hurler's arm, those who use the baffling delivery can pitch successfully in the big leagues up to the age of 50, as did Hoyt Wilhelm during his venerable career. The long-gone Washington Senators once had four knuckleball artists on the same pitching staff. They were a good, competitive ball club at the time. Paul Richards, one of the most innovative managers in baseball history, devised an oversized catcher's mitt that enabled receivers to funnel the unpredictable flutterballs into those gloves.

Phil Niekro, who pitched into baseball's version of old age, compiled in excess of 300 victories relying on the mystifying "dancer". Niekro and his brother Joe, also a proponent of the knuckleball, combined for 529 victories. While most pitchers don't experiment with the knuckler until they're professionals, Phil used it to dispose of enemy batters while still in high school. Thrown properly and with vital wind resistance, a knuckleball often breaks three times en route to the plate. It's difficult to control, hard to catch, and very tough to hit.

Against a hurler who relies almost exclusively on the knuckler, a hitter should set up far forward in batter's box, close to the plate and drastically reduce his swing. The pitcher should never aim for the corners. The technique is to aim for a target straight down the middle, then rely on the unpredictable movement of the ball to baffle and bedevil the hitter.

Former Los Angeles Dodgers' knuckleballer, Tom Candiotti, told me he's never fearful of throwing the pitch, even with a runner at third and the score tied in the ninth inning, when one errant delivery could cost him the ball game. He won't submit to fear even if he's not sure where the ball is headed when he turns it loose.

Managers have used knuckleball pitchers as starters and/or relievers. Clint Courtney, a big league catcher in the fifties and sixties, made a specialty of handling pitchers who threw the knuckleball. Curious to hit against the knuckleball, I once persuaded Al Papai, who pitched for both the Cardinals and Browns, to serve me some of the baffling pitches at Houston's Buff Stadium. He took a bucket of baseballs to the mound one sweltering summer day and I swung at perhaps fifty of his pitches. I can assure you I didn't solve the mystery of how to hit a knuckleball, although occasionally my bat at least made contact with the maddeningly deceptive pitches.

Athletes' hot streaks are always exciting. Joe Altobelli, a strong pull hitter, once crashed eight home runs in seven games while zeroing in on the "short porch" in Rochester's Silver Stadium. It was only 315 feet from home plate to the right field foul pole and only 360 feet to the right center field power alley. Altobelli would look for a pitch on the inside of the plate and concentrate on lifting the ball. Five of his eight home runs won games, either in the ninth inning or extra innings for the Red Wings.

Jacksonville outfielder, Mike Shannon, once cracked out seven hits in eight at bats in a double-header against Rochester. Shannon was immediately summoned to the major leagues and never looked back. I announced only one of Nolan Ryan's minor league games when he was a teammate of Tom Seaver and Jerry Koosman in Jacksonville. Ryan relieved for three innings, faced the minimum of nine batters and fanned EIGHT of them. I never witnessed a more dominant performance by a pitcher.

It's always exciting to follow and root for a team in the process of forging a long winning streak. I learned that as a 12-year-old in Chicago when the 1935 Cubs won 21 consecutive September games. They came from far back in the pack to overhaul the St. Louis Cardinals "Gas House Gang", clinching the pennant just one day before season's end. Talk about running the table!

Many years later, I visited with Cub hero, Phil Cavarretta, who blasted a home run off Paul Dean in St. Louis that put the rampaging Bruins on top two days before the season expired.

Or how about the 1938 Cubs, who on Labor Day found themselves 8 ½ games behind Pittsburgh? The never-say-die Cubs, who were making a practice of winning the pennant every third year (1929, 1932, 1935, and 1938) finally overhauled the Pirates when catcher/manager, Gabby Hartnett, blasted his historic "Homer in the Gloaming" to sink the Buccaneers. Chicago first baseman, Rip Collins, who had arrived from St. Louis a season earlier, told me an amusing story about that dramatic game.

Pittsburgh had seized a commanding lead before the Cubs roared back. With the bases loaded, Hartnett summoned Tony Lazzeri to pinch-hit. Lazzeri, winding up a storied career after being cut loose by the Yankees, hadn't played in so long that as he strode from the dugout he felt compelled to ask for directions. Collins was the on-deck hitter. Above the roar of the crowd, he heard Lazzeri inquire, "Hey, Rip, where in Hell's home plate?"

Lazzeri then slammed a base clearing double into the right field corner and the noise was deafening. I had special reason to remember that battle when Hartnett hit his game winning home run just before the umpires would have called the game due to impending darkness. On Labor Day, when the Cubs seemed hopelessly behind the Pirates, I made what I considered to be a safe bet against a Cub fanatic. I gave him 10-1 odds, my ten dollars against his dollar, that the Cubs wouldn't catch Pittsburgh. I was betting money I didn't have. Ten dollars in 1938 was a princely sum. So I rooted hard AGAINST my once beloved Cubs so I could collect the easy dollar. It served me right for sacrificing my loyalty for mercenary reasons.

I've been an inveterate and voracious reader of the sports page. One of my all time favorite lines was composed in 1945 by Warren Brown a waggish Chicago sports columnist. It focused on the upcoming Cubs-Tigers World Series. Summing up his analysis, Brown opined, "I don't see how either team can win."

Not all of those I admired were in uniform. The most entertaining public address announcer I ever heard was the Chicago Cubs', Pat Pieper, who seemed to have served in

CHAPTER 26: KNUCKLES & KNUCKLEHEADS

that capacity from time immemorial. He began his long stint using a megaphone before the advent of sound systems. He continued for decades with his microphone in a more technological age.

It's a wonder he lasted so long without being beheaded by a rapidly traveling foul ball. These days, all major league public address announcers operate from the press box area. Not Pat Pieper. He was on the grass at Wrigley Field, seemingly no more than 35 feet behind the batter's box, directly in front of the screen. He had to have been blessed with lightning quick reflexes to dodge foul balls. Pat was as much a fixture at Clark and Addison Streets as the ivy- covered walls.

I remember watching a Cubs-Cardinals double header when the weather was cool at the outset, then warmed up as brilliant sunshine prevailed. A couple of women fans doffed their coats and draped them over the left field wall, whereupon Pat, in that familiar and commanding voice, barked out, "Attention! Attention, please! Will the women sitting in the first row of the bleachers inside the left field foul pole, PLEASE REMOVE YOUR CLOTHING! Thank you." Whereupon the Wrigley Field multitude howled its collective approval.

27 MR. NOBODY & MR. OCTOBER

There are many who decry expansion baseball. With the Rockies and Marlins in '93 and two more teams in '98 many claim expansion has watered down the quality of play. It was expansion, however, that gave more athletes the chance to play; many became stars. Also consider the career minor leaguer who receives an opportunity to play in the big leagues and exceeds all expectations.

A case in point was the Colorado Rockies', Mike Kingery. In 1994, Kingery, 33, had reached a crossroads in a career that had been largely undistinguished. It was spent mostly in the minors, save for a few periods when he failed to make a strong impression at the major league level with different organizations. He seemed to be on the threshold of retirement inasmuch as he experienced a mediocre year with Omaha in the Kansas City organization in 1993.

Kingery was a non-roster player during the Rockies' Cactus League exhibition games in 1994. The Rockies were searching for a left handed hitter who could be inserted in the outfield for defensive purposes in late innings. Kingery failed to hit .200 during spring training. But he still made decent contact, could play all three outfield positions and as a veteran left-handed batter. He impressed manager Don Baylor just enough to survive the final cut. When Ellis Burks, acquired from the White Sox, bolted to a blazing start, chances for Kingery to play were rare.

Suddenly the picture changed. Burks suffered a fractured wrist when checking his swing, virtually ending his season. Baylor had no alternative but to insert Kingery into the regular lineup. Taking full advantage of unexpected opportunity, Mike seized the moment and went on a batting tear that lasted the remainder of the strike-shortened season. He also demonstrated surprising extra-base power. Defensively, there wasn't a better outfielder in the league. Kingery covered a vast amount of acreage in the huge area extending from the left-centerfield alley to right-center field at Mile High Stadium. Had Kingery not produced so extraordinarily, the Rockies would never have remained in the Western Division championship race as long as they did. The Rockies stayed with Los Angeles and San Francisco until Andres Galarraga sustained a broken hand in late July. Kingery helped the team to a playoff spot in 1995.

So much has been written about the lengthy strike that wiped out a considerable portion of the 1994 season and, shame of shames, the 1994 playoffs and World Series. The key word as I see it is, "WASTE." It was a waste of rare talent that doesn't last long. Baseball also wasted a great opportunity to entertain its millions of fans who long for the excitement of the post season.

I wonder if Tony Gwynn could have become the first player since Ted Williams in 1941 to reach the magical .400

batting mark? Could the Expos have held onto their lead and perhaps turned that moribund franchise around? Sadly, we'll never know.

All through the painful strike, it seemed to me the word compromise was conspicuously lacking. Sincere negotiations also seemed to be an important missing factor. As one observer sagely put it during one of baseball's darkest hours, "The strike is a battle between millionaires and multi-millionaires."

So many people who had come to rely on baseball were severely hurt. This included restaurant owners and employees near the ballparks and hotels that house huge travelling parties of visiting teams and out-of-town fans. Consider the plight of ushers and vendors for whom baseball is an important part of their livelihood. The list of people hurt by the strike goes on and on. I'm sure that in many major league cities some businesses were forced to shut down, even permanently, as a result of the accursed baseball strike.

Owners and players should be partners, not adversaries. The sport has magnificent rewards for all involved. Despite culpability on both sides, it would be foolhardy to condemn all owners and all players. One owner who did his utmost in continuing attempts to negotiate with the Player's Association was Jerry McMorris of the Colorado Rockies. He always demonstrated a willingness to hear the players' side and always worked towards compromise. McMorris has had a world of experience in labor negotiations and always has been a voice of reason. Since major league baseball came to Denver, McMorris' stature has risen among fellow owners and players alike.

Lack of a permanent commissioner in the 90's subjected baseball to ridicule. To have had an owner, Milwaukee's Bud Selig, operate in the role of temporary commissioner defied all logic. The commissioner, by the very nature of what the job was originally intended to be, should represent owners AND players. All of his actions and rulings should stem from whatever is "best for baseball." When Selig was named commissioner on a permanent basis he had to surrender his role in the Milwaukee Brewers' operation. One excellent suggestion I've heard is that half of the commissioner's salary should be paid by owners, the other half by the Players' Association. That would insure the commissioner's allegiance to both sides; something that has been sorely lacking.

The New York Yankees played the Colorado Rockies in the final 1995 replacement player exhibition games just before the long strike ended.

I spotted Reggie Jackson, working with some young hitters. When he had a free moment, I introduced myself and told him I would like to interview him. "Mr. October" seemed friendly enough, then proceeded to stare at me before observing, "Joe, I'd say you've been around a loooong time!"

I asked him about playing for disciplinarian football coach, Frank Kush, at Arizona State. Jackson was a good running back. Reggie remembered he didn't like it at the time, but playing for Kush toughened him. He referred to Kush as a father figure dedicated not only to football, but also to his players.

Reggie recalled what a great baseball mind Charlie Finley had and how he could easily have been an outstanding general manager. Elaborating, Jackson pointed out that Finley knew team chemistry, he appreciated the importance of getting rid of the ball quickly, he knew foot speed and bat speed and could read talent.

Inevitably, the conversation got around to the historic day when he walloped three consecutive World Series homers in the Yankees' clinching victory over the Dodgers in 1977.

I observed that many talented players let the adrenaline rush get out of hand to the point where they can't deliver on the grand stage of the World Series. Jackson said he keyed himself up, "then I worked on keying myself down," intensely concentrating on hitting the ball hard, making solid contact.

One of his historic homers was hit off knuckleballer, Charlie Hough. It seemed to me that would be an extraordinary achievement since the hitter has to generate his own power in connecting with the flutterball pitch. Reggie countered by saying he hit "about 8 or 9" home runs off knuckleball pitcher Wilbur Wood during his career.

Jackson is now a Hall of Famer and remains the only player in baseball history to have connected for five home runs in a World Series. Furthermore, he did it in just six games.

After talking with Reggie Jackson, I sought out Claire Smith of the New York Times to congratulate her on a masterfully written biography of Don Baylor. New York Post writer, Tom Keegan, heard the conversation and a startled look came over his face. He told me, "I recognized your voice. You were a boyhood hero of mine when you broadcast the games in Rochester, New York."

There was a special reason why Keegan was shocked to hear me. On a previous trip to Rochester, my name came up in a group of sports fans. The question was posed, "Has anyone ever heard from or about Joe Cullinane?"

A voice piped up, "Sorry to say, fellas, but Joe Cullinane PASSED AWAY!"

When Keegan heard me conversing with Claire, he envisioned a perfect POST story about my "comeback," accompanied by the headline, "Back from the dead!" Whereupon I reflected I at least deserved the Comeback of the Year Award.

28 THE BUSINESS OF BROADCASTING

Shifting from sport to sport when doing play-by-play, particularly when seasons overlap, presents a challenge. I've broadcast an afternoon football game, followed by a baseball game hours later. Baseball obviously has a more leisurely tempo, so the announcer matches the pace, pausing frequently when the action slows down. Football is a "stop and go" assignment for a broadcaster. The trick is to go smoothly from rapid, sometimes complex action to down time prior to the next play. That gives the broadcaster time for "housekeeping", such as informing listeners of substitutions entering the game, the score, time left in the quarter, down, yards to go, and precisely where the ball is on the field.

Whether doing play-by-play or interviews, it's important not to get too technical. The worst mistake a broadcaster can make is to speak over the heads of his listeners. Your audience won't complain if occasionally you delve into a game's finer points as long as you explain clearly and keep in mind that your audience isn't wholly comprised of experts.

The swift-paced tempo of basketball and hockey force the announcer to focus intensely in order to keep pace with action. Often the broadcaster must work substitutes into a game while rapid action continues, such as in hockey, when teams change lines on the fly. It's another reason why an announcer must do vital pre-game memory work, clearly associating in his mind the connection between name and number. When doing play-by-play, there is no time to glance at the scorebook to determine the names of numbers 17, 16, and 23.

With interviews, you sometimes encounter rude guests. Former St. Louis Cardinals' great, Enos Slaughter, splattered tobacco juice on my shoes when I interviewed him, then pretended it was an accident.

I had comfortable relationships with NBA coaches like Doug Moe, Billy Cunningham, Frank Layden and others. Pat Riley would personally line up players I wished to interview. I didn't hit it off at all with Don Nelson when he coached the Milwaukee Bucks. He willingly agreed to be interviewed, then gave sarcastic, condescending answers to some of my questions.

I once encountered an irritating situation when interviewing Kareem Abdul-Jabbar. He consented to do the interview but when I paused routinely to give the cutaway commercial cue, interrupting our conversation for but a few seconds, Jabbar casually strolled away. He had to be aware we needed to continue our discussion.

Dan Issel was standing nearby, ready to join his Nuggets teammates for a game day shoot around. I explained the situation to Issel and he gladly finished the interview. We designed our conversation solely around Dan's many head-to-head duels with Jabbar, so listeners probably never suspected that Kareem had essentially deserted me. I interviewed Jabbar several times, but he was never a very enthusiastic guest. He was fully capable of exuding charm, but never demonstrated it toward me. So be it. It was not my role to reinvent personalities.

I've always been irritated by announcers who don't prepare. All broadcasters make mistakes, inadvertently mispronouncing even a familiar name, for example. Announcing the wrong score is something that can happen to anyone. But failure to prepare, tedious though it sometimes may be, is inexcusable. It's an insult to the listening audience that is committed to giving the announcer time and attention. Ex-athletes, in particular, can be notorious offenders when it comes to lack of preparation.

What's involved in preparation for a broadcast? It's not all that complicated. Study statistics and trends. Talk to players, managers and coaches including those on opposing teams. Reading newspapers in your hometown and from other cities is a must. Out-of-town newspapers can be found on the internet. The announcer should do everything possible to familiarize himself with individuals on both teams. He should have enough discipline to set a schedule that allows him to be fully prepared for the broadcast.

A challenge I've always relished while doing play-by-play, is to get it right the first time.

As the late Denver Broncos voice, Bob Martin, once observed, "The play-by-play announcer isn't equipped with an eraser."

A baseball announcer must always be aware that what he says between plays is often more critical than describing action. He must also be cognizant of a constantly changing audience during the game.

Certain information must be periodically repeated, such as the score, the inning, base running situation, defensive alignment, count on the batter, on-deck hitter, bullpen activity, if any, and, for late comers, occasional reviews of how earlier scoring took place. Keep reminding your audience if the batter is left-handed or right-handed, or if he switch-hits. Tell your listeners if a pitcher is left or right-handed. It all sounds elementary, but it's important to keep the listening audience informed. Particularly in the late innings of close games, the announcer should feel free to anticipate strategy, such as when a bunt, an attempted steal or a hit and run play would be in order. Baseball includes a great deal of strategy and anticipation. It behooves the announcer to keep listeners in the game. Your word picture can be comprehensive, but make it easy to visualize.

Use significant stats to embellish a broadcast, but not dominate it. Excessive use of numbers is invariably deadly.

Whether it's play-by-play or interviews, an announcer must listen to his tapes. You must be your own harshest critic if you're to improve. On interviews, repeatedly ask yourself whether you're making the guest comfortable. Don't anticipate your next question. Be guided by what the guest has just said.

It's important the interviewer doesn't ask questions that can produce a simple yes or no answer. That can kill an interview. As much as you might admire the achievements of a certain guest, always keep in mind you're an equal during the conversation. Don't place anyone on a pedestal.

CHAPTER 28: THE BUSINESS OF BROADCASTING

Finally, have fun. You should be enjoying the job and if you do it rubs off on the audience. I've always prided myself in injecting the element of excitement into my broadcasts. After one of my basketball broadcasts, an enthusiastic listener recounted his reaction.

"My boy and I were lying on the floor eating popcorn and listening to your broadcast. Next thing I knew he was throwing popcorn at me. Before you could blink an eye, I was throwing popcorn at HIM." I don't think the woman of the house shared their enthusiasm.

I mentioned that we all make mistakes such as giving an incorrect score or saying the side has been retired even if there are only two outs, or mispronouncing a popular player's name. Don't attempt to cover up your mistake, which typically results from a lack of concentration. Tell the listener of your mental lapse, preferably in a light-hearted manner. Listeners never mind a bit of self-deprecating humor.

If you are on the air for any length of time and choose to ad-lib commercials, you are bound to insert foot in mouth on occasion. I've committed more than my share of faux pas' in this regard. White Owl Cigars once sponsored a segment of my Rochester Red Wing baseball broadcasts. Discarding the script of a commercial I thought was too long to squeeze in during the time allotted, I proceeded to do a shortened ad-lib version and was doing splendidly until time came to recite the slogan.

It was a simple slogan in which I was to refer to their product as "America's Most Expensive Ten Cent Cigar." White Owl was justifiably proud of the slogan and derived considerable mileage from it. But in my haste I inadvertently urged my listeners to, "Light up a White Owl and enjoy America's most EXPLOSIVE ten cent cigar?" I don't know whether cause and effect came into play but White Owl's sponsorship was missing the following season.

All of us in the media should guard constantly against over-reliance on cliches. They can have an irritating effect on an audience. We're all tired of, "taking it one game at a time".

Even a nickname can essentially become a cliche. Baseball players, in the friendliest of manner, often greet me with "Hey, big guy." I'm convinced that even Bill Veeck's diminutive, Eddie Gaedel, if he were still around, would be greeted in precisely that manner.

Do sons of broadcasters (a different kind of SOB) have it easier? How about Harry Caray, son Skip and Skip's son Chip. It's certainly reasonable to assume that being Harry's son paved the path for Skip to receive his chance. But the fact remains he has made the most of opportunity. Same thing when you're talking about Thom Brenneman, son of the Cincinnati Reds' Marty Brennaman. Thom severed his play-by-play assignment with the Cubs, and is now the leading voice of the Arizona Diamondbacks.

The late Jack Buck's son, Joe, who assisted his dad on Cardinals broadcasts, is another rising young star in sports broadcasting. He has further distinguished himself on network playoff broadcasts and as an NFL play-by-play man. When Jack, a revered figure, passed away in 2002, Joe continued to grow as the Redbirds top play-by-play announcer.

The brothers Albert have written one of television and radio's most successful stories. Marv has long announced

NBA games, along with NFL play-by-play assignments. He also did hockey broadcasts on the New York Rangers' network. Unflappable on the air, he has won many awards for sportscasting excellence. Al was an outstanding Denver Nuggets broadcaster for 15 years and did boxing on the USA network and Steve once described Indiana Pacers basketball games. The three brothers (real name Aufrichtig) all had broadcasting ambitions from early boyhood. They even set up improvised facilities in the family basement in Brooklyn.

If offspring of accomplished sports broadcasters don't measure up, they are soon gone in this highly competitive field. Certainly "who you know" counts. Ex-athletes and coaches often receive lucrative TV and radio assignments even when they are not initially ready. They're permitted to learn on the job, something that would never occur but for their immediately recognizable names.

Nepotism might be preferable to some baseball broadcasting partnerships that never should have been formed. The Cleveland duo of Jimmy Dudley and Bob Neal would be a prime example. Bill O'Donnell told me when he went into Cleveland as a Baltimore announcer, he noticed that while Neal was on the air, Dudley could be observed reading a book. When Dudley's turn came, the roles were reversed. It got so bad that Indians' General Manager, Gabe Paul, felt he had no recourse but to fire one of them. He chose to hand Dudley a pink slip.

Red Barber never made a secret of his feuds with upstart, Joe Garagiola. There was a noticeable absence of chemistry when Milo Hamilton worked alongside Harry Caray in the Cubs' booth. With baseball in particular, it's an untenable situation when announcers don't mesh with each other. There are so many games and so many hours on the air that listeners and viewers sense when tension exists.

Finally, a sports announcer should pay close attention to his mail, particularly if it's critical. If the writer is absolutely unreasonable, then the broadcaster can quickly deposit the correspondence in the nearest wastebasket. Other times the writer might make some valid points. One letter I particularly remember was written in red ink and began in this manner:

"Dear Joe, if you look as bad as you sound, you must really be ugly."

The tone of the letter didn't exactly improve as I continued to read.

EPILOGUE

And what is currently happening in the life of your storyteller? I still live in Denver with my wife, Ottie. Our sons, Pat and Mike, live in the Denver area as well.

Not long ago Ottie and I took a sentimental journey back to Rochester for a wonderful visit with daughter, Susie, her husband, Dale Rath, and our ever-energetic grandchildren, Brian and Paul.

I was inducted into the Rochester Red Wings' Hall of Fame, along with the storied Earl Weaver and long time office administrator, Pat Santillo. Susie and Dale hosted a fun-filled party and we saw my two brothers, Mickey and Jack, Mickey's wife Dorothy, and many friends from those long ago days in upstate New York. Earl and Marianna Weaver came to our party and it was a warm feeling indeed to renew acquaintances. Two years spent with this feisty warrior of so many baseball battlegrounds are among my most cherished memories. It had been 21 years since our last get-together.

During the induction ceremonies that evening, as we walked down the first base line toward home plate, Earl sounded like a puppy dog yipping at my heels. I still can hear that urgent, gravelly voice, "Come on, Joe. Don't talk too long. Keep it short. I've got a hook and if you go too long, I'm coming out to get you."

Of course, I heeded Earl's sage advice after Joe Altobelli introduced me. You can imagine the surge of excitement I felt a year later when Weaver was inducted into the Baseball Hall of Fame in Cooperstown.

As I reflect upon sportscasting, I fervently hope I'm still a part of that fascinating world for many years to come. I can't help but think that some very talented young sportscasters must even now be abandoning the business. It is a nerve jangling, never ending musical chairs job, particularly play-by-play, and the vagabond way of life it so frequently entails. To those who do persevere and continue to pursue their dreams, good luck and God Speed.

I've kept my hand in radio with a sports interview program in Denver. There is an abundance of human interest content in the programs and a wide range of subject matter.

Like James Michener creating another epic novel, a persuasive lawyer arguing his case in court, a clergyman delivering a sermon to his flock, or, perhaps, like a surgeon performing an operation, I'm still a broadcaster. For, you see, THIS IS WHAT I DO!